THE BEST

of

THE WEST OF IRELAND

The Bedside Book of the West of Ireland

PADRAIC O'FARRELL

THE MERCIER PRESS
DUBLIN and CORK

The Mercier Press Limited
4 Bridge Street, Cork.
25 Lower Abbey Street, Dublin 1.

ISBN 0 85342 644 9

To Aisling

Printed by Litho Press Co., Midleton.

Foreword

The west of Ireland has always had a particular fascination for the native Irish and visitor alike. Its mountains, valleys, rivers, lakes and seaboard boast a visual and intellectual beauty and every acre echoes a legend, every stone a piece of history. Its towns are modern, yet they serve hinterlands which still, happily, cling to many of the old ways and customs and continue to preserve tradition.

That unique combination of attitudes is, hopefully, reflected in this anthology which presents a variety of writings from an area that holds a special place in a world which is experiencing unprecedented turmoil and which is in need of the tranquillity still attainable in the west of Ireland.

Acknowlededgments

I wish to thank most sincerely the following for the use of copyright material: The Mercier Press and its authors: James N. Healy, John M. Feehan, Maureen Jolliffe, Séamas Ó Buachalla, Desmond Maguire. I thank also the Head of the Department of Irish Folklore, University College Dublin; Walton's Ltd., Dublin; Editor *Leitrim Guardian;* Director and Staff, National Library; Librarian and staff, Longford-Westmeath Library. I thank my wife, Maureen for her proof-correction and my family for their continuing patience.

I have taken every precaution to ensure that no copyright material has been included without the necessary permission. In the unlikely case of any inadvertent departure from this intention I would request copyright-holders to contact me, please.

Padraic O'Farrell

1. THE GALLANT OLD WEST

While you honour in song and in story the names of the
      patriot men,
Whose valour has covered with glory full many a mountain
      and glen.
Forget not the boys of the heather, who marshalled their
      bravest and best,
When Eire was broken in Wexford and looked for revenge
      to the west.

Chorus: I give you the gallant old west, boys.
          Where rallied our bravest and best
        When Ireland lay broken and bleeding;
          Hurrah for the men of the west!

The hill tops with glory were glowing, 'twas the eve of a
      bright harvest day,
When the ships we'd been wearily waiting sailed into
      Killala's broad bay;
And over the hills went the slogan, to awaken in every
      breast
The fire that has never been quenched, boys, among the
      true hearts of the west.

Chorus

Killala was ours 'ere the midnight, and high over Ballina
      town
Our banners in triumph were waving before the next sun
      had gone down.
We gathered to speed the good work, boys, the true men
      anear and afar;
And history can tell how we routed the redcoats through
      old Castlebar.

Chorus

And pledge me 'The stout sons of France', boys, bold
      Humbert and all his brave men,
Whose tramp, like the trumpet of battle, brought hope to
      the drooping again.

Since Eire has caught to her bosom on many a mountain
    and hill
The gallants who fell so they're here, boys, to cheer us to
    victory still.
Chorus

Though all the bright dreamings we cherished went down
    in disaster and woe,
The spirit of old is still with us that never would bend to the
    foe;
And Connaught is ready whenever the loud rolling tuck of
    the drum
Rings out to awaken the echoes and tell us the morning has
    come.
Final Chorus: So here's to gallant old west, boys,
                Who rallied her bravest and best,
            When Ireland was broken and bleeding;
              Hurrah, boys! Hurrah for the west!

2. NATURAL WONDERS

The mountains are on either side pouring down their
supplies in rivers, broad or narrow, but ever rapid, and
rushing over, or around, huge rocks that divert their
channels, so that each is twisted into singular forms before
it reaches the plain upon which we are now traversing. Immediately 'at the turn down to Maam' is one of the most
beautiful and picturesque of these lakes, Lough Anillaun
— The Lake of many Islands — surrounded by thick under-
wood, and full of small islets on which the furze, broom,
and heather flourish luxuriantly. On the right is the western
bank of Lough Corrib; and occasionally striking and agree-
able views are caught of this great sheet of water. On the
left is the noble mountain of Shanfiola, rising high above a
score of lesser hills, and looking down upon the loveliest,
yet the loneliest, of all lakes—Lough Inagh; lying in solitary
grandeur in the centre of a circle of hills, each impassable,
except to the pedestrian, or to one of the little sure-footed
ponies, that are never known to stumble, and will bear

THE HOTEL AT MAAM

almost incredible fatigue, although fed only upon the thin herbage of the boggy soil, and looking so poor and wretched that a hill-blast would seem sufficient to upset them. Yet these ragged-coated steeds not uncommonly journey forty miles without other refreshment than the 'drain' of oatmeal and water. We have been travelling upon the road made by the justly celebrated engineer, Mr Nimmo — one of the benefactors of Ireland, who civilised this wild district; and as we approach Maam, we arrive in sight of the cottage built for his accommodation while superintending his 'works'. It is now the Maam Hotel, and stands beside an elegant bridge which crosses an arm of Lough Corrib, where the lake is joined by the river Bealnabrack.

At Maam, then, the tourist must rest. He is in the midst of a host of natural wonders; within reach of all the leading beauties of the district; and he will be domiciled at a very comfortable inn.

There was nothing in Connamara that astonished or delighted us more than this valley, through which the river winds at the base of a double line of mountains. We saw many scenes of wilder and more rugged grandeur, but none that so happily mingled the sublime and beautiful. We are here, indeed, in the presence of the 'lone majesty of untamed nature'; few of the works of man appear around us — of habitations there are none, except a score of humble cabins sheltered by the overhanging hill: and of the labours of the husbandman the evidence is very scanty:—

> No fields of waving corn were here,
> Vineyard, nor bowering fig, nor fruitful vine—
> Only the rocky vale, the mountain stream,
> Incumbent crags, and hills that over hills
> Arose on either hand. Here hung the yew—
> Here the rich heath that o'er some smooth ascent
> Its purple glory spread—or golden gorse—
> Bare here, and striated with many a hue
> Scored by the wintry rain, by torrents here,
> And with o'erhanging rocks abrupt.
> Here crags loose hanging o'er the narrow pass
> Impended.

The peculiar beauty of the scene consists, indeed, in the happy blending of rugged grandeur with gentle beauty; for the river moves calmly through the dell, after having rushed in torrents down the sides of the mountain, and pursues its even course into the broad lake. Of this remarkable scenery, the appended sketch may convey some idea. Only one solitary ruin is within our ken—the ivy-crowned walls of an old castle, classed among the oldest in Ireland, which occupies a low island close to the shore of Lough Corrib.

3. KINCORA

Oh! where Kincora! is Brian the Great?
  And where is the beauty that once was thine?
Oh, where are the princes and nobles that sate
  At the feast in thy halls, and drank the red wine?
    Where, oh, Kincora?

Oh, where Kincora! are thy valorous lords?
  Oh, whither, thou Hospitable! are they gone?
Oh, where are the Dalcassians of the golden swords?

And where are the warriors Brian led on?
        Where, oh, Kincora?

And where is Morrogh, the descendant of kings?
    The defeater of a hundred—the daringly brave—
Who set but slight store by jewels and rings—
    Who swam down the torrent and laugh'd at its wave?
        Where, oh, Kincora?

And where is Donogh, King Brian's worthy son?
    And where is Conaing the beautiful chief?
And Kian and Core? Alas! they are gone—
    They have left me this night alone with my grief!
        Left me, Kincora!

And where are the chiefs with whom Brian went forth,
    The ne'er vanquished sons of Erin the brave,
The great King of Onaght, renowned for his worth
    And the host of Baskinn from the western wave?
        Where, oh, Kincora?

Oh, where is Duolann of the Swift-footed Steeds?
    And where is Kian, who was son of Molloy?
And where is King Lonergan, the fame of whose deeds
    In the red battle-field no time can destroy?
        Where, oh, Kincora?

And where is that youth of majestic height,
    The faith-keeping Prince of Scots? Even he,
As wide as his fame was, as great as was his might,
    Was tributary, oh Kincora, to thee!
        Thee, oh, Kincora!

They are gone, those heroes of royal birth,
    Who plundered no churches, and broke no trust;
'Tis weary for me to be living on earth
    When they, oh Kincora, lie low in the dust!
        Low, oh, Kincora!

Oh, never again will Princes appear
  To rival the Dalcassians of the Cleaving Swords.
I can never dream of meeting, afar or anear,
  In the east or the west, such heroes and lords!
    Never, Kincora!

Oh, dear are the images my memory calls up
  Of Brian Boru! — how he never would miss
To give me at the banquet, the first bright cup!
  Ah! why did he heap on me honour like this?
    Why, oh, Kincora?

I am Mac Liag, and my home is on the Lake;
  Thither often to that place whose beauty is fled,
Came Brian, to ask me, and I went for his sake,
  Oh, my grief! that I should live, and Brian be dead.
    Dead, oh, Kincora!

4. ON THE HIGH SEAS

Graunya Uaile had no sooner recognised the Spanish build
than she resolved to fling her galleys upon the monster, for
all his bulk and gun metal. Her own weather-beaten little
flag-ship had already crept its way through the treacherous
windings of her place of ambush, when to her rage she saw a
barque running down channel straight for the distressed
battle-ship. Her galleys lay as secret as sharks behind a
rocky breakwater, and as vigilant. The great yellow stand-
ard of Spain was suddenly unfurled from the frigate. The
barque bore straight ahead and displayed no ensign until
the blaze of a broadside told her business. The contest
between the guns of the towering frigate and those of the
barque seemed madness; but the barque was the *Judith*
which had soared into the epic by its prowess in the Island
Voyage, and its master Ebenezer Jewell, was one of the
foremost of the buccaneers who had filled the Spanish
world with terror of the English fire-drakes.
  The Spanish cannoneers made terrific play upon their

small assailant, but on pressed Jewell, spitting fire undauntedly back. The Inishcleir galleys stole seawards under cover of a farther headland. Through the smoke of the cannonade and the spray which still tossed in shattered clouds between sea and sky, Graunya Uaile saw a tongue of fire burst out and leap up higher and stronger. The barque had caught fire. With flames around him and the raking guns in front, Jewell bore straight ahead with unwavering helm until he was within grappling reach of the frigate. Before the astounded Spaniards' eyes, his men swarmed over the side on their desperate boarding venture, letting the blazing barque drift untenanted to leeward. Jewell's desperation carried all before it. The Spanish cannoneers could but strike back wildly with their linstocks when they were hurled from the place-of-arms in the waist, stunned and bleeding, and the English buccaneers pressed on, with eyes as fearful as their pike-thrusts, to the forecastle and the battery at the poop.

With the glistening eye of an eagle watching from his cliff, Graunya Uaile spread her wings and swooped.

'Now, boys, for the laun-bwilla (the brain blow)!' she cried. 'With one stroke you can baulk the Socsanach and spoil the Spaniard. Down on them, and take your fill of vengeance and of silver, both!'

The men, who cowered before the imaginary Edge of the World, felt their blood kindle and throb at sight of the real battle-ship. A land wind, and their sheaves of oars, like the quilled wings of sea birds, shot the galleys forward into the haze.

The Spaniards, once recovered from their amazement, fought desperately from castle to treasure-room. Their gallantry was legible in a bloody track of writhing bodies. But Jewell's sword raged like a curse of Eliseus among the Moabites, and his young gentleman lieutenant, Ryppingale, who had rushed from school afire for the adventures of Drake and Raleigh, cut his way through deck and cabin with the relish of some Homeric tussle in the playfields.

The struggle on deck was long over. Some of the victors were binding their prisoners; others were slaking their thirst with draughts of Spanish wine; others, again, were tearing open with hatchets the ship's cupboards, and feasting their eyes upon the dazzling wells of silver in the hold. Suddenly there was heard overhead something that paralysed the buccaneers with terror.

'It is witchcraft! Hell hath broke loose to the rescue of the idolaters!' whispered the Puritan pirates, more superstitious than the Catholic ones. With their thunder shouts of 'Ab-ab-oo!' the O'Maelias were swarming over the sides and clinging to the rigging. A few bewildered buccaneers who scrambled to the stairheads saw blood-shot eyes of fire blazing at them out of forests of black hair, and — saw nothing more in this world.

5. HOMELAND

Far away from the land of the shamrock and heather
In search of a living, as exiles we roam.
But whenever we chance to assemble together,
We think of the land where we once had a home.
But these homes are destroyed and our soil confiscated,
The hand of the tyrant brought plunder and woe;
The fires are now quenched and our hearts desolated,
In our once happy homes in the County Mayo.

Long years have now passed since with hearts full of sorrow,
The land of the shamrock we left far behind;
But how we would like to go back there tomorrow;
To the scenes of our youth, which we still bear in mind;
The days of our childhood, it's now we recall them.
They cling to our vision wherever we go;
And the friends of our youth we will never forget them,
They too are exiled from the County Mayo.

From historic Killala, from Swinford to Calla,
Ballyhaunis and Westport and old Castlebar,
Kiltimagh and Claremorris, Belmullet and Erris,
Kilkelly and Knock that's famed near and far;

Balla, Ballinrobe, Ballina and Bohola,
Keeloges and Foxford a few miles below
Newport and Cong with old Straide and Manulla,
Charlestown too, in the County Mayo.

Then on with the cause 'till our aim is accomplished,
Those who would fault us are cowardly and mean,
So stop in the fight 'till the tyrant is vanquished
And expelled from our dear little island of Green.
With the foes of our land we have fought a long battle,
Soon they will get their last death-dealing blow,
When old 'Nick' has received them, their brains he will
     rattle,
For the wrongs they have done to the County Mayo.

From Galway to Dublin, from Derry to Kerry,
New York and 'Frisco and Boston also,
In Pittsburg, Chicago, Detroit and Toronto,
There are stout-hearted men from the County Mayo.
Now boys, pull together in all sorts of weather
Don't show the white feather, wherever you go,
Act each as a brother and help one another
Like true hearted men from the County Mayo.

6. ELECTION ADDRESS

I once again appeal to the voters of every shade of politics
and religion in Co. Clare, I now do so with very mixed feelings. You saw I had a tough time in 1944 to get even the fifth
seat, though I had given the use of their limbs to people of
every class in Co. Clare, without fee or reward, and I never
asked to what party any of them belonged when they came
to me.

But now when I want their No. 1 votes, I have to go on
my knees almost to beg their votes off them. I do not at all
think that treatment fair especially when I thought I had
earned their votes and gratitude. It is very disappointing
when I find people so ungrateful as to forget what I have

done for them when they were no use to themselves or to anybody else; only a bundle of shattered bones.

Now, when they can do their daily work, surely I should expect a simple stroke of a pencil — that is the only compensation I ask or get.

There are thirteen candidates for four seats. But I hold I have done more lasting good for the people of Clare than all the others combined. I do not fear contradiction when I say I have done more for the people of Clare than the Gaelic Athletic Association, Fianna Fail, Fine Gael, Clann na Talmahan, Clann na Poblachta and Labour Party. It remains to be seen what gratitude and votes I will get at the forthcoming Election.

I need hardly tell you that I am sincerely grateful for the votes I get, as a great many vote for me whom I never did a turn for. Hoping you will be true to yourselves and to me by giving me your No. 1 votes.

As ever,

The same old Bonesetter,

Thomas Burke,
Miltown Malbay.

7. CLONMACNOISE

In a quiet water'd land, a land of roses,
    Stands Saint Kieran's city fair;
And the warriors of Erin in their famous generations
    Slumber there.

There beneath the dewy hillside sleep the noblest
    Of the clan of Conn,
Each below his stone with name in branching Ogham
    And the sacred knot thereon.

There they laid to rest the seven Kings of Tara,
    There the sons of Cairbrè sleep—
Battle-banners of the Gael that in Kieran's plain of crosses
    Now their final hosting keep.

And in Clonmacnoise they laid the men of Teffia,
  And right many a lord of Breagh;
Deep the sod above Clan Creidè and Clan Conaill,
  Kind in hall and fierce in fray.

Many and many a son of Conn the Hundred-fighter
  In the red earth lies at rest;
Many a blue eye of Clan Colman the turf covers,
  Many a swan-white breast.

8. CONG

To this Abbey, which retains many tokens of early splendour, Roderick O'Conor, the last of the Irish kings, retired
when his English enemies grew too strong for him; here he
passed the remainder of his life, living in monastic seclusion
for fifteen years; and here, according to tradition, he was
buried. The honour of covering his remains is, however,
disputed by Clonmacnoise. But, at least, the place of his
interment is pointed out at Cong by village historians, who
would as soon part with their birthright as relinquish their
claim to the dust of the latest monarch of their country. The
grave stands immediately under the great east window;
common stones are heaped in careless profusion above it;
but it is surrounded by very perfect and beautiful sculptured buttresses, doorways, and ornaments of a gorgeous
character, which speak of the former wealth and power of
this sanctuary of kings. The sceptical as to the interment of
O'Conor, will, however, receive ample assurance that
here, at all events, the last abbot—Prendergast—was
buried about twenty years ago. He died at the age of eighty-
eight; and his memory is revered by rich and poor in the
neighbourhood; he was described to us as a fine white-
headed man, the very picture of benevolence, who had
been followed, for upwards of half a century, by blessings
wherever he passed. A model of the Irish priest of the old
school he was, who combined the manners of a gentleman
with the accomplishments of a scholar.

It is impossible to render justice to the rich remains of this famous abbey: the entrance gateway we have pictured; it is in a very perfect state, and is but a sample of the whole of the interesting structure. The windows are, in especial,

AT CONG

curious specimens of decorated Norman architecture; and some of the carvings seem as fresh, after the lapse of centuries, as if they had but recently passed from the hands of the sculptor. The situation is also exceedingly beautiful; the site was happily chosen; and in walking round the old walls and in the garden, or standing beside a singularly clear well that oozes from a rock, it is difficult not to

Envy them — those monks of old.

The Cross of Cong, of which we append an engraved copy, was presented to the Royal Irish Academy in 1839, by Professor McCullagh, by whom it had been purchased from

THE CROSS
OF CONG

the Roman Catholic clergyman of Cong, who with the
funds thus supplied was enabled to repair his chapel, which
had been unroofed by a storm. It is 'a most interesting
memorial of the period preceding the English invasion, and
shows a very high state of art in the country at the time
when it was made, which was the early part of the twelfth
century, under the reign of Therdelach Ua Conchovar (or
Turlogh O'Conor), father of Roderick. This date is supplied by the Gaelic inscriptions, extremely clear and well
cut, which cover the silver edges of the cross, and which,
besides giving the names of the king and of a contemporary
dignitary of the church, preserve that of the artist himself,

21

who was an Irishman. A Latin inscription informs us that it contains a precious relic — a portion of the wood of the "true cross"; and this circumstance will account for the veneration in which it has been held for ages, though, unfortunately, it was not sufficient to protect it from injury, much of the ornamental work having been removed, and part of the inscriptions torn away. Notwithstanding these depredations, however, it is still a splendid monument of ecclesiastical antiquity. In the centre of the arms, at their junction with the shaft, there is a fixed cruciform piece of oak, marked with the figure of a cross, and much older, apparently, than the rest of the wood, which is oak also. This piece bears marks of the knife, as if it had been taken for the relic; though it is perhaps too large to be so, and, besides, it does not appear that the true cross was made of oak. Hereabouts, however, the relic certainly was; for the place is surmounted by a very conspicuous crystal of quartz, not long, but round, being in fact a thick, double-convex lens, with one surface much more convex than the other. The cross is studded "full of precious stones", or rather imitations of them, disposed at regular distances along the edges, and elsewhere. The central crystal is surrounded by an elegant ornament in gold; and all the rest of the cross, both before and behind, is richly adorned with an interwoven tracery, of that peculiar kind which the Irish were so fond of. "The tracery is of solid gold;* the inscribed edging is of silver; and both are separated from the wooden frame by plates of copper"; the whole being held together by nails, of which the heads are little heads of animals. The shaft also terminates below, in the double head of an animal, which is large and very finely executed. The end is hollow, to admit a staff, by which the cross was carried, like the crozier of an archbishop. The height of the shaft is about two feet and a half, and the span of the arms about nineteen inches.'

* This has been since found to be a mistake; the gold is a wash very well put on, indeed nothing can be better. How it was done would puzzle a modern artist; altogether the gold on the cross is not worth ten shillings,

9. O'CONOR'S GRAVE

Clear as air, the western waters
Evermore their sweet, unchanging song
Murmur in their stony channels
Round O'Conor's sepulchre in Cong.

Crownless, hopeless, here he lingered;
Year on year went by him like a dream,
While the far-off roar of conquest
Murmured faintly like the singing stream.

Here he died, and here they tombed him,
Men of Fechin, changing round his grave.
Did they know, ah! did they know it,
What they buried by the babbling wave?

Now above the sleep of Rury
Holy things and great have passed away;
Stone by stone the stately Abbey
Falls and fades in passionless decay.

Darkly grows the quiet ivy,
Pale the broken arches glimmer through;
Dark upon the cloister-garden
Dreams the shadow of the ancient yew.

Through the roofless aisles the verdure
Flows , the meadow-sweet and fox-glove bloom.
Earth, the mother and consoler,
Winds soft arms about the lonely tomb.

yet it is made to go very far, and may have been intended more for use than
ornament — to prevent the brass becoming foul from the dampness of the
climate. During our visit to Maam in 1852, we obtained a ring that had
been found at Cong; it is of iron, but has marks of having been coated with
gold.

Peace and holy gloom possess him,
Last of Gaelic monarchs of the Gael,
Slumbering by the young, eternal
River-voices of the western vale.

10. HEN'S CASTLE

The castle of *Caislean-na-circe* or the Hen's Castle, is said
to have originated with Roderick O'Conor, the last of the
native kings, as a place of refuge and safety in the event of
his enemies forcing him from the sanctuary of neighbouring
Cong. It is, however, asserted that 'its true founders were
the sons of Roderick, assisted by Richard de Burgo, Lord
of Connaught, and Lord Justice of Ireland.' That an object
thus situated—having no accompaniments around but
those in keeping with it—should, in the fanciful traditions
of an imaginative people, be deemed to have had a super-
natural origin, is only what might have been naturally
expected; and such, indeed, is the popular belief. If we
inquire of the peasantry its origin, or the origin of its name,
the ready answer is given, that it was built by enchantment
in one night by a cock and a hen grouse, who had been an
Irish prince and princess!

The Hen's Castle is not without legendary traditions con-
nected with its history anterior to its dilapidation; the
following outline of one of these—and the latest—as told at
the cottage firesides around Lough Corrib, may be worth
preserving as having a probable foundation in truth.

It is said that during the troubled reign of Queen Elizabeth, a lady of the O'Flaherty's, who was an heiress and a
widow, with an only child, a daughter, to preserve her
property from the grasp of her own family and that of the
De Burgos, or Burkes, shut herself up with her child in the
Hen's Castle, attended by twenty faithful followers, of tried
courage and devotion to her service, of her own and her
husband's family. As such a step was, however, pregnant
with danger to herself, by exciting the attention and alarm
of the government and local authorities, and furnishing her

24

THE HEN'S CASTLE

enemies with an excuse for aggression, she felt it necessary to obtain the Queen's sanction to her proceedings; accordingly she addressed a letter to her Majesty, requesting her permission to arm her followers, and alleging, as a reason for it, the disaffected state of the country, and her ardent desire to preserve its peace for her Majesty. The letter, after the fashion of the times, was not signed by the lady in her acquired matron's name, but in her maiden one, of which no doubt she was more proud; it was Bivian or Bivinda O'Flaherty. The Queen received it graciously; but not being particularly well acquainted with the gender of Irish Christian names, and never suspecting from the style or matter of the epistle that it had emanated from one of her own sex, she returned an answer written with her own hand, authorising her good friend 'Captain Bivian O'Flaherty' to retain twenty men at her Majesty's expense, for the preservation of the peace of the country; and they were maintained accordingly, till the infant heiress, becoming adult, was united to Thomas Blake, the ancestor of the present Sir John Blake, of Menlo Castle, and proprietor of the Castle of the Hen.

Another legend is, that O'Flaherty, the cock, being slain in an encounter by the Joyces, they thought to get easy possession of his castle: but his widow defended it bravely and successfully, and was hence called *The Hen*. One other legend we borrow from the Rev. Caesar Otway:—

The place was called Castle Hen, and all the neighbours said that it was built by a witch, who came there one night when the Joyces were driving the old residenters, the O'Flahertys, out of the country; and she appeared on the little island with a black hen following her, which all allowed must not be natural; but, at any rate, before morning, up sprung that great building. And then she gave it to King O'Flaherty, and the hen along with it; and she told him to take good care of the hen, for that when the Sassenach besieged him, and with their boats would be keeping off all provisions from him, the black hen would lay white eggs enough to keep him from starving; and so it was. The Joyces often besieged it, and tried, when they could not take it by force, to starve out the O'Flaherty, but the eggs kept him alive. But sure enough, one Easter Sunday, after a long Lent, the master, poor man, was mighty craving for a bit of meat, and, indeed, I suppose the poteen had got into his head; any how, he couldn't be in his right mind, for he takes the hen, do you see, cuts her throat, boils her for his dinner—and a heavy dinner it was for him; for, from that day forth he had neither luck nor grace; the Joyces soon surrounded the place with their boats —not a morsel of meal or meat would they let near it; and you see that, as the black hen was no more, he could have no eggs, and then he had to give up the last hold of the O'Flahertys in this place; he had to quit before the Joyces, and go to the wild country.

11. THE DOG OF AUGHRIM

'The day is ours, my gallant men!' cried brave, but vain St
    Ruth;
'We've won a deathless victory for Liberty and Truth;
We'll wrest the land from William's grasp though we're but
    one to three,
We'll make his crew remember long the Pass of Urrachree.

26

That though with myriad cannon they poured the fierce
      attack,
Still with valour and the naked sword thrice have we flung
      them back.
They're beaten, boys! they're beaten! still unsheath your
      swords again,
And — on them like an an avalanche! and sweep them from
      the plain.

Like thunderbolt upon the foe the Irish column sped.
Athlone's deep stain to wash away — St Ruth is at their
      head.
On! onward rolls that wave of death; but, God! what means
      this cry,
St Ruth the brave sits on his charger headless 'neath the
      sky.

Oh! where's the gallant Sarsfield now, is victory defeat?
O, God! in mercy, strike us dead; 'twere better than
      retreat.
Oh! where is Limerick's hero brave? the chiefless soldiers
      cry,
And scorning flight they wait the dawn to give them light to
      die.

No quarter! was the slogan of the Williamites that day —
And graveless lay the murdered brave to dogs and thieves
      a prey;
But even dogs more sacred held the dying and the slain,
Than Ginkle and his hireling hordes on Aughrim's bloody
      plain.

When Saxon fiends the scene of death and robbery had fled
An Irish wolf-dog sought his lord 'mid heaps of pilfered
      dead,
And strove with more than human love to rob death of its
      prize,
Then moaned a dirge above his breast and kissed his lips
      and eyes.

The summer sun shone fiercely down upon the corpse-
      strewn plain,
Where bird and beast of air and field devoured the naked
      slain;
Yet faithful still that wolf-dog stood 'mid savage growls and
      groans,
To guard alike from man and beast his well-loved master's
      bones.

When autumn pencilled summer's bloom in tints of gold
      and red,
And winter over hill and dale a ghostly mantle spread,
The weird winds wailed across the moor and moaned
      adown the dell —
Yet guarded well that noble dog his master where he fell.

Spring timidly was glancing down upon the spreading plain,
Where seven months death's sentinel the faithful dog had
      lain,
When carelessly across the moor an English soldier trod
And halted near the only bones remaining on the sod.

Up sprang the faithful wolf-dog, he knew a foe was near,
And feared that foe would desecrate the bones he loved
      so dear;
Fierce and defiant there he stood, the soldier, seized with
      dread,
Took aim, and fired — the noble dog fell on his master —
      dead.

12. O'ROURKE COUNTRY

Early next day we left Carrick for Leitrim village, which is
only a short distance away. The morning mist was still
haunting the banks of the river, but the sunshine was breaking through and beginning to warm the earth. We made our
way through the narrow wandering river, its banks tapes-

tried with green, until we finally tied up at the wharf below
Leitrim Bridge. This small village is steeped in history. It
was from here the tragic Dervogilla left her cruel husband
and eloped with Dermot MacMurrough. This is all
O'Rourke country and in the sixteenth century one of the
O'Rourkes, to show his contempt for Queen Elizabeth,
tied an effigy of her to his horse's tail. He was later arrested
and executed in London for this act. He refused to recog-
nise the court or ask for mercy. His only request was that he
be hanged with a halter made of withy, which was used to
hang Irish peasants, rather than with English hemp. His son
Brian O'Rourke was taken by the English while still a child,
and educated at Oxford, Hampton and Middle Temple.
When it was thought he was a young Englishman he was
asked to return to Ireland and influence his clan to give
allegiance to the British crown. The proud youth refused
and so was imprisoned in the Tower of London where he
died thirty years later. The O'Rourkes were ultimately
driven from their lands and they fled to the continent. In
modern times one of them became Bishop of Danzig. He
was forced to leave that city when it was occupied by the
Nazis and it was reported later that he was murdered by the
Russians. Leitrim was also the final home of the great
O'Sullivan Bere after his long winter march from Cork. He
left with one thousand souls and when he arrived here only
thirty-five were still alive.

13. INVITATION FROM A CRAGLEA, KILLALOE NYMPH

Listen, whilst I in truthful numbers tell
What wonders next, these hardships o'er, befell;
I lay possess'd by many a gloomy thought,
When lo! a lovely nymph my presence sought;
Her long hair waving in its downward flow,
Her bright cheeks warming with the berry's glow,
Her form, her gait, her ev'ry limb so fair
Told me 'twas Aevall of Craglea was there.

Upon my aching brow she laid her hand,
And gently raising, whisper'd me to stand:
Then soaring upward drew me thro' the night,
Till on a verdant plain she stay'd her flight.
A gloomy cave whence noxious vapours gush
Its shaggy sides o'ergrown with heath and bush,
Fearing I saw, and marvell'd to what end .
The banshee next her wandering steps would bend.
She saw my trouble, and with kindly speech,
'Fear not,' she said, 'No pain or harm shall reach
Thy head from aught thou see'st nor stand aghast
At fiend or monster, they shall all be past
In safety, so thou bide with me and thou shalt say
Thou saw'st a sight which no man to this day
Of Thomond's clan's e'er saw, or shall see more,
When thou returnest full of wondrous lore...'

14. THE SPIRIT OF SOLDIERING

In days gone by when 'taking the shilling' or joining the
British Army was commonplace, an Ennistymon man found
himself fourpence short in his weekly pay. The old cry 'I'll
soldier no more' escaped his lips when he complained to the
paymaster. All he received was the customary official
reply, 'We'll see what we can do about it in your next pay
packet.' The Ennistymon soldier wasn't easily put off, however, and he demanded an interview with his company
commander.

He got no satisfaction there either so he went through all
the channels—commanding officer, brigadier-general,
adjutant-general. The latter promised him that he would get
the fourpence in his next pay packet but the soldier said he
would desert if he didn't get it there and then.

He was granted an interview then with the chief-of-staff
of the combined forces, a man that held the rank of Lord.
'The Lord be praised,' said the chief, 'but you're the man I
need. If you sleep in the huge house on the edge of my estate for three nights in a row, you'll get your fourpence.'

Well three days wasn't as long a wait as a week so the soldier consented. He didn't sleep much in the house, however, for an almighty row went on upstairs. Indeed the soldier at one stage called to the revellers to come down and have the 'hoolie' in his room. He felt that if he was to be kept awake by spirits he might as well have a good time.

The racket was worse on the second night but the soldier was in no way afraid. On the third night the noise was worse again. What's more, he was rudely interrupted by a bull bearing a coffin impaled on his horns. The coffin was deposited beside the soldier. He opened it and an old man sat up and asked for a smoke. When the soldier gave him a filled pipe, the rude corpse threw it away. Unabashed, the soldier threatened him that if he hadn't manners he would kill him — or do whatever equivalent is done to impudent corpses!

The threat worked, the corpse had its smoke and then lay back peacefully in its coffin. A young man then came into the room and decorated the soldier — at least he gave him a letter for the Lord chief-of-staff.

The Lord read the letter which promised that the house would remain peaceful thereafter. It also promised a crock of gold for the Lord, one for the soldier and one for Masses for the young man who, it transpired, was the Lord's son. The Lord went to where the letter said the gold lay. Such was his delight that he offered the soldier his own crock of gold in addition to what was promised to him. He also told the soldier that he would make an officer out of him.

Perhaps this is what put him off but in any event the soldier replied:

'I want nothing of what you offer. All I want is my four-pence— *now.*'

15. THE DEATH OF O'CÁROLAN

There is an empty seat by many a board,
A guest is miss'd in hostelry and hall—
There is a harp hung up in Alderford

That was, in Ireland, sweetest harp of all.
The hand that made it speak, woe's me! is cold,
The darken'd eyeballs roll inspired no more;
The lips—the potent lips—gape like a mould
Where late the golden torrent floated o'er.

In vain the watchman looks from Mayo's towers
For him whose presence filled all hearts with mirth;
In vain the gather'd guests outsit the hours—
The honour'd chair is vacant by the hearth.
From Castle Archdall, Moneyglass and Trim,
The courteous messages go forth in vain;
Kind words no longer have a joy for him
Whose final lodge is in Death's dark demesne!

Kilronan Abbey is his castle now,
And there, till Doomsday, peacefully he'll stay.
In vain they weave new garlands for his brow,
In vain they go to meet him by the way;
In kindred company, he does not tire—
The native dead and noble lie around;
His life-long song has ceased, his wood and wire
Rest, a sweet harp unstrung, in holy ground.

Last of our ancient minstrels! thou, who lent
A buoyant motive to a foundering race—
Whose saving song, into their being blent,
Sustained them by its passion and its grace:
God rest you! may your judgment dues be light,
Dear Thorlogh! and the purgatorial days
Be few and short, till clothed in holy white,
Your soul may come before the throne of rays.

16. WHERE THERE'S A WILL. . .

I. . . bequeath my body to be buried in Ffenagh Church. I
leave my wife Russell Reynolds alias Ware during her life
my manor of Loughscur and the twenty cartrons of land as

it was granted to my father and to me by general Letters Patent from His Majesty. She shall have the disposal of the rents etc. until the next May after her death *(sic.)*, and then my son and heir, James, is to enjoy the said Manor of Loughscur. I leave to my said son and heir. . . my parsonage of Manteroly in Co. Leitrim. I give to my son James my interest in the manor of Laghin. . . except the quarter of Laghin which I leave to my son William Reynolds. My cozen Henry Fitzwilliam Reynolds. . . My daughter Katherine ten shillings because she married without my consent. . .

17. A BALLAD FROM ATHENRY

In the year of 1880, to Connaught I came in;
I left my native Donegal, a fortune for to win,
But instead of winning fortune, 'twas myself I brought to
      ruin
For day and night my thoughts were set on the maid of
      River View.

When I came here a stranger, my heart was light and gay;
I did my work with a right good will and I got a generous
      pay.
I was faithful to my master and his work well I did do,
And when my day's toil was over I set out for River View.

When first I saw this maiden fair 'twas on a summer night;
She was standing at her father's door just like an angel
      bright.
My heart at once was captured and my fate was sealed,
      I knew —
Come weal or woe, I'll love no one but this maid from River
      View.

I courteously saluted her, she answered with a smile;
As I was at my leisure, we chatted for a while.
And when I turned to leave her, she raised her eyes so blue
And said 'I hope you'll call again some night to River View.'

For many evenings after that we met and had a walk;
We'd stroll down by the river and of our love we would talk.
I told her how I loved her and I vowed that I'd be true
If she'd come with me to Donegal and leave sweet River
    View.

She looked at me so sadly, gently clasped my hand and said:
'Tis true I love you dearly but we never can be wed.
My father's lands are mortgaged and for them I am a pawn,
I am plighted to your master and must marry him next fall.

I saw her home that evening and we sadly said goodbye;
She looked quite brokenhearted as she slowly passed me
    by.
I left for Donegal next day with a broken heart 'tis true,
And I bade adieu forever to Caraun and River View.

Now all young men who hear this tale a warning take by me;
Don't be too quick to fall in love when a pretty maid you
    see.
For if you do, you'll surely rue, the truth I tell to you,
For she'll steal your heart and leave you like the maid of
    River View.

18. THE HARP OF THE WOOD

There is a Wood in the west of Connacht that is called the
Great Wood. Another name that it has is the Old Wood.
And not without cause has that name been given to it, for it
is the oldest Wood in Ireland. Of living things or of dead
things, there is nothing in the land of Fal older than that
Wood except the grey stones of the hills and the lamentable
sigh of the old sea. If the Bens of Beola have mind and
memory they can scarcely remember an age when that
Wood was not. It was there before the Bens received their
own name. It was there, a deep and mysterious forest,
when Beola took the westward Connacht way as he drew
towards the sod of his death. If Beola had any name for it, it

is not likely that he called it by any other name than that of the Old Wood.

There was a time when the Bens themselves were not. Beann Bhán was a plain, Beann Chorr was a smooth and level lowland, Dubh-Chruach was perchance a glen; or it may be that in the place of the glorious Bens were gravel and white sea-sand, with the lamentable sigh of the sea for ever above them. 'Let the Bens be lifted up,' said the Artisan of the World, and at that word fires broke from the womb of the earth, and one by one they reared the rugged head of Dubh-Chruach, and the naked side of Alt na gCaorach, and the majestic awful bulk of the lasting Bens. Bare were the grey flagstones in the beginning of time and rough and fearsome were the shoulders of the hills, but it was not long until their flanks were clad with the woodland mantle of the cool forest. Whence did ye come, O primal seeds of the Old Wood? What path or way did ye take? Did the fowl of the air carry you hither in their breasts, or did the vociferous laughing winds scatter you here with invisible hands? Who appointed unto you this wilderness for your place of meeting and trysting? I hail that Being, and I hail you, O seeds from which sprang the Wood that I have loved!

From east and west and north and south, from every airt from which a wind blows, by every aerial path that bird follows, they came answering their tryst: seed of the oak, seed of the birch, seed of the yew, seed of the sally, seed of the rowan, seed of the holly, seed of the rugged Irish larch. And each seed of them grew into a tree, and each tree produced after its kind, until there rose the towering ponderous oaks and the lovely dappled-lightsome birches, and until hard holly and Irish larch waxed strong, and every tree of the trees of the wood according to its season. Then was heard in the loneliness of the desert a new music answering the ancient music of the sea, to wit, the Harp of the Wood playing very sweetly, very sadly, whenever its strings were plucked by the invisible fingers of the wind.

That music was heard throughout the wilds proclaiming to the many tribes of the air and the earth that there was a haven of refuge and a dwellingplace for them in the shade of the foliage of the young Wood. They answered the summons. The grey badger came and the brown white-toothed otter, the red fox and the grizzled wolf, the tree cat and the pine marten and the little red squirrel, the russet deer and the roebuck, the hare and the stoat and the spiny hedgehog, the old black rat and the little grey mouse, and every furtive timid thing that loves the woodland; the great boar came and declared war upon the clans of the Wood until they did homage to him and called him king; there came various and wonderful flocks of birds, and innumerable hosts of creeping things, and multitudinous swarms of bees and ants and chafers and flies, so that at the end of time there was not a hole or hollow or cavern, a river bank or a lake shore, a wave of water or a knoll of earth, a tree or a bush or a shrub, a stalk or a leaf or a slender rib of grass in all the greenwood that was not the homestead and the fortress of some creature of the woodland creatures.

A long time passed away. Ireland put her first bareness off her. The Old Wood remained a wood. Another time passed away, a very long time. Ireland put her second bareness off her. The Old Wood remained a wood. A third period of time elapsed. One day that came there was heard a new and terrible sound in the Wood: the measured heavy blows of an axe. For years those blows were heard. Full much of the timber of the Old Wood was cut down. The shoulders of the Bens and the hollows of the glens were once more left bare. But all the trees were not cut. Duhb-Chruach remained a wood. Ireland is passing through her third bareness, but that much of the Old Wood is woodland still. Dubh-Chruach and the glen beneath it and the borders of the lake that is in the middle of the glen: that much is still a Wood, and will be a Wood until the Day of Doom. Small though it be today, the Old Wood is there after all the ages, it and the lives it holds, like a little world in itself. I hail you, O steadfast, ever-living seeds of the Old Wood!

19. GRÁINNE MHAOL

There's sorrow at our mother's heart, her eyes are dim
      today,
For all the cherished dreams she nursed are vanishing
      away.
There are vacant seats by many hearths, and from all sides
      comes the tale,
That the true and brave fly o'er the wave from dear old
      Gráinne Mhaol.

When the homestead rose in the olden time and the thin
      blue smoke upcurled;
Where reigned the smiles that made our isle the gem land
      of the world;
'Tis the stranger's cow is grazing now, and the bodach, cold
      and pale
Usurps the place of the ancient race who loved old Gráinne
      Mhaol.

At the Sunday mass, where the neighbours met and talked
      their tidings o'er,
But little's left of all the throng that used to crowd the
      door.
A few grey heads, a few hot hearts at fortune's frowning
      rail,
But scarce a face with will to chase the grief from Gráinne
      Mhaol.

For doubt sits brooding on the hill; despair stalks through
      the glen;
And not a voice goes through the land to rouse her earnest
      men.
Have all the memories of the past forsaken town and vale,
That not a hand in all the land is raised for Gráinne Mhaol?

Oh! shame, if even one survives to point the way to dawn,
That men should fear to tread the path the true and brave
      have gone!

Oh! bitter shame that feud should sap the strength that
      could prevail
O'er fraud and might, to chase the night of woe from
      Gráinne Mhaol.

Have all the hopes our fathers held been handed down in
      vain?
Must all the thoughts that cheered their lives be never
      known again?
Must silence fill the fields and fairs and coming ages hail
Forgotten graves, unthinking slaves, as the meed of
      Gráinne Mhaol!

No, no! across the thund'ring waves the answer rings full
      high;
No, no! re-echoes many a heart beneath the Irish sky;
The land shall wake; her exiled sons across the seas shall
      sail
Once more to set a coronet on loved old Gráinne Mhaol!

20. RACES OF CASTLEBAR

    Allons, enfants de la patrie!
    Le jour de gloire est arrivé!
    Contre nous de la tyrannie
    L'étendarde sanglant est levé.

What place has such a language in a book on the west of
Ireland? Well the verse was accompanied by 'Yeroos' and
'Mo Gradh Thú' as Irishmen accompanied and guided
General Humbert's French army of eight hundred men
from Ballina to battle with General Lake at Castlebar.
More French had been expected at Killala, where they
landed, for the Irish rebellion of 1798 was almost suppress-
ed. But Napoleon had decided that Egypt needed his
armies more than Ireland. General Sarrazin had already set
out for Castlebar when Humbert spoke thus to Colonel
D'Arcy:

> . . . I have distributed proclamations broadcast,
> calling attention to the wrongs of Ireland and announc-
> ing that we have come, in the name of the French
> Republic, One and Indivisible, to their assistance and
> to establish Liberty, Equality and Fraternity, and to
> cement the efforts you Irish have already so bravely
> made to shake off an intolerable tyranny. . .

With Irish guides the force attacked Lake along an axis
which he considered impossible and against his five thousand strong defence supported by nine pieces of cannon.

The wiry blue-uniformed *tirailleurs* swarmed the hillside
firing their muskets with precision, their Irish pikemen
ready to participate when the enemy were closed with.
Brave D'Arcy was killed in the action but not before the
enemy lines broke. The wild war-cry of 'Connacht Abú,
Abú' rose from the pikemen. French and Irish pressed
home their attack and the British forces fled towards Tuam,
forty miles away. During the pursuit, called thereafter 'The
Races of Castlebar' all the English artillery was captured
and five pairs of their colours seized.

> '. . . And the boys will all be there
> With their pikes in good repair,'
> Says the Sean Bhean Bhocht.

21. SWEET MAYO

On the deck of Patrick Lynch's boat I sat in woeful plight,
Through my sighing all the weary day and weeping all the
      night.
Were it not that full of sorrow from my people forth I go,
By the blessed sun, 'tis royally I'd sing thy praise, Mayo.

When I dwelt at home in plenty, and my gold did much
      abound,
In the company of fair young maids the Spanish ale went
      round.
'Tis a bitter change from those gay days that now I'm forced
      to go,

And must leave my bones in Santa Cruz, far from my own
    Mayo.

They are altered girls in Irrul now; 'tis proud they're grown
    and high,
With their hair-bags and their top-knots — for I pass their
    buckles by.
But it's little now I heed their airs, for God will have it so,
That I must depart for foreign lands, and leave my sweet
    Mayo.

'Tis my grief that Patrick Loughlin is not Earl in Irrul still,
And that Brian Duff no longer rules as Lord upon the Hill;
And that Colonel Hugh McGrady should be lying dead
    and low,
And I sailing, sailing swiftly from the county of Mayo.

22. CORMAC MAC AIRT

His hair was slightly curled and of golden colour; he held a
scarlet shield with engraved devices and golden hooks with
clasps of silver; a wide-folding purple cloak on him, with a
gem-set gold torque around his neck; a girdle with golden
buckles and studded with precious stones upon him; two
golden network sandals with golden buckles upon him; two
spears with golden sockets and many bronze rivets in his
hand; while he stood in the full glow of beauty without
defect or blemish.

23. FAMINE

Weary men, what reap ye?—Golden corn for the stranger.
What sow ye?—Human corpses that wait for the avenger.
Fainting forms, hunger stricken, what see ye in the offing?
Stately ships to bear our food away, amid the stranger's
    scoffing.

There's a proud array of soldiers—what do they round
　　your door?
They guard our master's granaries from the thin hands of
　　the poor.
Pale mothers, wherefore weeping? Would to God that we
　　were dead—
Our children swoon before us, and we cannot give them
　　bread.

Little children, tears are strange upon your infant faces;
God meant you but to smile within your mother's soft
　　embraces.
O, we know not what is smiling, and we know not what is
　　dying;
But we're hungry, very hungry, and we cannot stop our
　　crying.
And some of us grow cold and white—we know not what it
　　means;
But, as they lie beside us, we tremble in our dreams.
There's a gaunt crowd on the highway—are you come to
　　pray to man
With hollow eyes that cannot weep, and for words your
　　faces wan?

No; the blood is dead within our veins—we care not now for
　　life;
Let us lie hid in the ditches, far from children and from
　　wife;
We cannot stay and listen to their raving famished cries—
Bread! Bread! Bread! and none to still their agonies.
We left our infants playing with their dead mother's hand:
We left our maidens maddened by the fever's scorching
　　brand:
Better, maiden, thou wert strangled in thy own dark-
　　twisted tresses—
Better, infant, thou were smothered in thy mother's first
　　caresses.

41

We are fainting in our misery, but God will hear our groan;
 Yet, if fellow-men desert us, will He hearken from His
        throne?
Accursed are we in our own land, yet toil we still and toil;
But the stranger reaps our harvest—the alien owns our soil.
O Christ! how have we sinned, that on our native plains
We perish homeless, naked, starved, with branded brow
        like Cain's?
Dying, dying wearily, with a torture sure and slow—
Dying as a dog would die, by the wayside as we go.

One by one they're falling round us, their pale faces to the
        sky;
We've no strength left to dig them graves—there let them
        lie.
The wild bird, if he's stricken, is mourned by the others,
But we—we die in Christian land—we die amid our
        brothers,
In a land which God has given us, like a wild beast in his
        cave,
Without a tear, a prayer, a shroud, a coffin, or a grave.
Ha! but think ye, the contortions on each livid face ye see
Will not be read on judgment-day by eyes of Deity?

We are wretches, famished, scorned, human tools to build
        your pride,
But God will yet take vengeance for the souls for whom
        Christ died.
Now in your hour of pleasure—bask ye in the world's
        caress;
But our whitening bones against ye will rise as witnesses,
From the cabins and the ditches in their charred uncoffined
        masses.
For the Angel of the Trumpet will know them as he passes,
A ghastly spectral army, before the great God we'll stand
And arraign ye as our murderers, the spoilers of our land!

24. FAMINE SHIPS

Ships loaded with emigrants plied from Sligo during the years preceding the famine as well as after it. Grossly overloaded, the steerage passengers huddled together trying to provide food for themselves as the filth became unbearable. Disease was rampant and many captains and shipping-line owners were careless. Of 440 passengers on board the *Larch* which left Sligo in 1847, 108 died before reaching Quebec and another 100 died in quarantine having disembarked.

25. CHOLERA

The inhabitants of Sligo did not appear to me a healthy race; I thought I never saw so many sickly, pale-faced people. It is possible that fancy may have assisted this conclusion, having heard so much of the extraordinary visitation of cholera, which two years before threatened to depopulate the town. Nowhere, in Ireland, did cholera rage with such deadly violence as in Sligo; and I found in the town, when I visited it, the greatest dread of its re-appearance, a few cases having appeared at Ballina, and in some of the intervening villages.

26. MANHOOD

The men are big-bodied with handsome features and limbs, active and nimble as roe deers; they eat but one meal a day and that at night: their usual food is butter and oaten bread; their drink is sour milk, having none other they do not drink water which is best of all. . . They dress after their fashion with tight hose and short coats made of a very coarse goat's hair. . . They are great pedestrians and very enduring as regards to fatigue. . . They sleep on the ground on freshly cut rushes full of water and frost. The most of the women are handsome but ill-arranged.

27. MARY OF MEELICK

Long in lonely despair have I worship'd the dream,
   That brightens my heart with the glow of thy form;
Let my slumber's vision, my day's hallowed beam,
   Let it shine, my soul's treasure, to brighten and warm.
How can thy bosom be cold to the swell,
   Of the faith, the devotion, that's nurtured in mine;
Nay, my own love, let thy kindness dispel
   The clouds, and bid morning around me to shine.

In the sorrow, the anguish, that tortures my breast,
   I weep for the hour that endued it with life;
In thy sight alone, I have rapture and rest,
   Look down, my soul's love, on my spirit's dark strife.
Fly from the world, from its coldness, its guile,
   Oh fly to the breast, whose rich promise thou art;
Let not distrust ever shadow the smile,
   Chill the love that united us once heart to heart.

O'er the monument brightens the midsummer dawn,
   Where it looks from the west on the gush of the morn;
Through the wave bright forms wanton radiantly on,
   And the warren's grey flock the green valley's adorn.
The nuts thickly cluster; the bird to the day
   His shrill matin pours while it streams thro' his bower;
Blest is his lot, doomed in Meelick to stray,
   And to call thee his own, the bright vale's brightest flower.

Deeply shrined in my soul is thy image, dear maid,
   Thy lip's honied store—and thy cheeks summer glow;
And the tendril play of thy brow's sunny braid,
   And the sheen of thy neck like the sparkling of snow.
Light of my soul! what a transport for him,
   Through whose bosom can tremble each motion of thine;
My soul is enslaved—and my sight becomes dim,
   As I gaze on the riches my love must resign.

In yon bright distant isle, with my Mary to rove,
  To gaze on the amber of each glowing tress;
With each vow fulfilled and recorded above,
  Grant me this, fate hath nought that beyond it may bless.
Alas! cruel fair one—she heeds not my tears,
  And the truth I have cherished consumes me in vain;
Sorrow hath brought me the whiteness of years,
  The cold grave brings repose—let me rest in Killmain.

28. OLD CLADDAGH

'. . . The Claddagh, (an Irish word that signifies the sea-shore) is a village situated on the estate of Mr Whaley, near the strand, about a quarter of a mile to the west of Galway.

CABIN IN THE CLADDAH

45

It is irregularly built, but very extensive, and intersected into several streets. The number of houses or cabins, which are all thatched, was returned, in 1812, at 468, inhabited by 500 families, consisting of 1,050 males and 1,280 females but the population is now (1820) considerably grown, being supposed to exceed 3,000 souls.

It is a very ancient village, and, according to tradition, was the first residence of the settlers of this quarter; a circumstance not very unlikely, from its contiguity to the bay, and the consequent convenience for the purpose of fishing, which appears to have been their original occupation. Previously to 1808, the streets and exterior of this large village were as remarkable for want of cleanliness, as the interior of most of the houses was for neatness and regularity.

About that time Hurdis of the royal navy, then commanding the sea fensibles of this district, persuaded the fishermen to appropriate a small portion of their weekly pay for the purpose of paving and cleansing about their houses, and since that time it has been observed that they have got rid of many of those contagious disorders which generally prevail in large villages. . .'

29. CLADDAGH CLOTHES

'. . . Three flannel vests, under a fourth of which cotton or dimity, trimmed with tape of the same colour, over these a fine blue rug jacket with a standing collar and horn buttons, a blue plush breeches never tied or buttoned at the knees, blue worsted stockings, a pair of new brogues, a broad trimmed hat neither cocked or slouched, and a red silk handkerchief about his neck, completes the holyday dress of a Claddagh fisherman. At all other times they wear the common jacket and trousers usual with persons of their occupation. The women still retain their ancient Irish habit, consisting of a blue mantle, a red body-gown, a petticoat of the same colour, and a blue or red cotton handkerchief bound round the head after the old fashion.

On Sundays or festivals, however, they make a more

modern appearance; a matron's dress being generally composed of a blue rug cloak trimmed with fine ribbon, a rich calico or stuff gown, with the red flannel body-gown, however, occasionally worn over it, and a silk handkerchief on the head. . .'

30. THEY LOVED ME STILL

She said, 'They gave me of their best,
They lived, they gave their lives for me;
I tossed them to the howling waste,
And flung them to the foaming sea.'

She said, 'I never gave them aught,
Not mine the power, if mine the will;
I let them starve, I let them bleed, —
They bled and starved, and loved me still.'

She said, 'Ten times they fought for me,
Ten times they strove with might and main,
Ten times I saw them beaten down,
Ten times they rose, and fought again.'

She said, 'I stayed alone at home,
A dreary woman, grey and cold;
I never asked them how they fared,
Yet still they loved me as of old.'

She said, 'I never called them sons,
I almost ceased to breathe their name,
Then caught it echoing down the wind,
Blown backwards from the lips of Fame.'

She said, 'Not mine, not mine that fame;
Far over sea, far over land,
Cast forth like rubbish from my shores,
They won it yonder, sword in hand.'

She said, 'God knows they owe me nought,
I tossed them to the foaming sea,
I tossed them to the howling waste,
Yet still their love comes home to me.'

31. A LAMENT

You feeling hearted Christians I hope you will draw near
I'm sure this sad and shocking news will fill your heart with
      fear
For the murder of my lawful wife as you may plainly see
I'm condemned to suffer death upon the gallows tree.

Edward Walsh it is my name in Castlebar I did dwell
I own I had a virtuous wife I know she loved me well
Till the devil strongly tempted me the truth I now must say
Overpowered by his temptation I took her life away.

It was on a Sunday evening it became an awful night
When I followed her to the bake house it was to her a fright
I gave her deadly wounds for assistance she did call
But none came near to help her which proved her sad
      downfall.

She begged and prayed for mercy while struggling in the
      strife
Saying don't leave your children orphans, Ned spare me
      my life
But all she prayed it was in vain I'd hear her say no more
For with my deadly weapons I left her in her gore.

When the murder was discovered it caused a great surprise
To see her mangled body would draw tears from your eyes
Her limbs all bruised and broken I killed her in her bloom
May the Lord her soul receive she met a fearful doom.

The Police they were sent for and the house they did
      surround.

I then was taken prisoner and in irons strongly bound
I was sent to the assizes the judge my case to try
When I was marching off to jail my wife's funeral passed by.

When I was placed in the dock my trial for to stand
I thought I'd be acquitted by the Judges of the land
But the murder was terrific as you may plainly see
To heaven cried for vengeance which proved my destiny.

When the judge was passing sentence he spoke to me in
       grief
Saying make your peace with God you will get no reprieve
For the murder of your lawful wife you are condemned to
       die
On 19th day of August upon the gallows high.

The people of Castlebar her loss they do deplore
Likewise her friends and parents it grieves their heart full
       sore.
To see their child all in her prime to be laid in the clay
Now for the soul of Mary Walsh let every Christian pray.

Now my time will soon be spent I'm sorry for what I've done
I hope my pardon I will get as now my race is run
I own I used her cruelly it's the last I have to say
How will I dare to face my God upon the Judgment day.

32. CAPTAIN BOYCOTT

Lough Mask can claim to have given a word to the English
language for it was the estate of Lord Erne which had the
infamous Captain Boycott as its agent. That was in 1873 but
the astute man soon leased large tracts which he himself
farmed at a handsome profit. A rugged small man, he treat-
ed the tenants of the estate roughly. When they sought a
reduction of their rates in 1879 and it was not forthcoming
he was threatened with death. The Ballinrobe branch of the
Land League did not treat the threat seriously but they did

take up the tenants' case, particularly after a process-server was beaten away from the home of a tenant threatened with eviction.

There followed a fine example of the value of peaceful protest. The tactic had been recommended by Charles Stewart Parnell and was simplicity in itself. On 24 September 1880, local people, briefed by one Fr John O'Malley, arrived at Lough Mask House and ordered all employees of the estate, a formidable number, to leave. This they gladly did and Captain Boycott was left with a harvest to save and no labourers to help. Traders were also warned off supplying the 'Big House' and even the mail was cut off. Boycott, however, did manage to get off his letter to the Editor on a number of occasions and the events of the Mayo countryside became the talking point in fashionable houses abroad. *The Times* took up his case even as the Captain was being escorted about his business by members of the R.I.C. and Ulster Orangemen (led by a pair called Stoppard and Goddard). Newsmen converged on Claremorris whose innkeepers beamed with pleasure. Offers of help arrived from more and more Orangemen until the Government became alarmed and themselves despatched 'official' assistance, fifty labourers in all and a huge protection force of police and military. Trainloads of troops were boohed at stations along the way. Food and shelter were denied the arrivals, no transport was available to bring them to Lough Mask House. Mayo rain fell heavily as if in support of the hidden peasants who watched with glee as Her Majesty's Government's task force trudged through muddy roads to their destination.

Police, hussars, members of the 84th Regiment with fixed bayonets, pressmen and magistrates supported the fifty labourers saving the harvest over a period of fifteen days. Then they assembled for their departure and Fr O'Malley shouldered his umbrella as the soldiers shouldered their arms. He accorded the force a safe passage from his parish as he marched ahead of them, occasionally affording a mock reprimand to an old lady for attempting to harass the forces of the Crown.

The traditional system of the British Empire had been challenged by a handful of County Mayo tenants and the protest was an enormous success. Boycott left Lough Mask House and was even refused hotel accommodation in Dublin. He moved to England where he stayed for a mere ten months.

The Irish peasantry proved their unpredictability yet again when they accepted the Captain back among them — even showing him some respect.

33. THE CURSE OF CROMWELL

In trance I roamed that land forlorn
By battle first, then famine worn;
   I walked in gloom and dread.
The Land remained: the hills were there,
The vales—but few remained to share.
   That realm untenanted.

Far-circling wastes, far-bending skies;
Clouds as at Nature's obsequies
   Slow trailing scarf and pall:—
In whistling winds on creaked the crane,
Grey lakes upstared from moor and plain,
   Like eyes on God that call.

Turn where I might no blade of green
Diversified the tawny scene:
   Bushless the waste and bare:
A dusky red the hills, as though
Some deluge ebbing years ago
   Had left but seaweed there.

Dark red the vales: that single hue
O'er rotting swamps an aspect threw
   Monotonous yet grand:
Long-feared—for centuries in decay—
Like a maimed lion there it lay,
   What once had been a Land.

Yet, day by day, as dropt the sun
A furnace glare through vapours dim
   Illumed each mountain's head:
Old tower and keep their crowns of flame
That hour assumed; old years of shame
   Like fiends exorcised, fled.

That hour, from sorrow's trance awaking,
My soul, like day from darkness breaking,
   With might prophetic fired,
To these red hills and setting suns
Returned antiphonal response
   As gleam by gleam expired.

And in my spirit grew and gathered
Knowledge that Ireland's worst was weathered,
   Her last dread penance paid;
Conviction that for earthly scath
In world-wide victories of her Faith
   Atonement should be made.

That hour, as one who walks in vision,
Of God's 'New Heavens' I had fruition,
   And saw and inly burned:
And I beheld a multitude
Of those whose robes were washed in blood,
Saw chains to sceptres turned!

And I saw Thrones, and seers thereon
Judging, and Tribes like snow that shone
   And diamond towers high-piled,
Towers of that City, theirs at last,
Through tribulations who have passed,
   And theirs the undefiled.

A Land becomes a monument!
Man works; but God's concealed intent
   Converts his worst to best:
The first of Altars was a Tomb—

Ireland! thy gravestone shall become—
God's altar in the West.

34. BALLYMOTE BRIEFING

No fellowship with a king — no falling out with a madman
— no dealing with a revengeful man — no competition with
the powerful — no wrong to be done to seven classes of
people excited to anger, viz.: a bard, a commander, a
woman, a prisoner, a drunken person, a druid, a king in his
own dominions.

No stopping the pace of a going wheel by strength of
hands — no forcing the sea — no entering a battle with
broken hands — no heightening the grief of a sorrowful
man — no merriment in the seat of justice — no grief at
feasts — no oblivion in ordnances or laws — no contention
with a righteous person — no mocking of a wise man — no
staying in dangerous roads — no prosperity shall follow
malice — no coveting of skirmishes — a lion is not a safe
companion to all persons.

35. THE RENEGADE

Come all you gallant Galway boys,
    And I will tell you how,
Old Reddington the Renegade,
    Makes such a racket now;
'Twas in the year of Forty-eight,
    One blooming summer's day,
That noble William Smith O'Brien,
    Fell in the traitors way.

Oh! then this base informer,
    He vowed he'd lose a fall —
Or hold O'Brien's Carpet-bag,
    His letters, shirts and all!
And so he held his greedy grip,
    Until the trial came

And then he swore his life away,
    With infamy and shame.

Next came the cursed Titles Bill,
    With penalties and pains,
To send our holy Bishops,
    All across the seas in chains;
And then this upstart traitor,
    He said he'd lend a hand,
To banish them like serpents,
    From their own native land.

Is this 'the man for Galway',
    Accursed by man and God,
False to our holy Roman Church,
    And the green old Irish sod;
May Heaven Almighty strike us low,
    And Earth refuse us bread,
Ere this of gallant Galway's tribes,
    Should ever yet be said!

Then down with this false renegade,
    Him, and ribbon blue,
The recreant Knight of the Carpet Bag
    To honour so untrue;
From Ross bold Duffy hunted him.
    At home, for years to grieve,
And in the County — John of Tuam,
    Gave him his 'Ticket-of-leave'.

In old Kilcornan let him pine,
    His perfidy to rue,
And when he talks of Galway's men,
    Still raise the 'Wirrastrue';
Of us he ne'er shall make the means,
    To drive his traitor trade,
Hurrah for Galway's honour bright,
    And Down with the Renegade!

The history of Galway is full of interest—from the year 1178, when the Anglo-Normans first set hostile foot in Connaught, to the war of the Revolution, when the town surrendered, upon honourable terms, to the victorious Ginkle, who had previously routed the Irish forces at Aughrim. During all the terrible contests of centuries, Galway had its ample share of glory and grief; participating largely in the persecutions of the several periods, but maintaining a high character for courage and probity throughout. Of its old strength as a fortified town, there are few remains; but of its former wealth and splendour, as compared with other towns of Ireland, there are many—they exhibit, generally, tokens of the commercial habits of the people rather than of their military character. Nearly every lane and alley contains some token of their grandeur; and over the doorways of a very large number of the dilapidated houses are still standing the armorial bearings of the early occupiers. So remarkable, indeed, are those bits of Spain transferred to the wild west of Ireland, that Mr Inglis, who had visited the former country a short time previous to his tour in the latter, thus refers to the resemblances he observed between them: 'I had heard that I should find in Galway some traces of its Spanish origin, but was not prepared to find so much to remind me of that land of romance. At every second step I saw something to recall it to my recollection. I found the wide entries and broad stairs of Cadiz and Malaga; the arched gateways, with the outer and inner railing, and the court within—needing only the fountain and flower vases to emulate Seville. I found the sculptured gateways, and grotesque architecture, which carried the imagination to the Moorish cities of Granada and Valencia. I even found the little sliding wicket for observation in one or two doors, reminding one of the secrecy, mystery, and caution observed, where gallantry and superstition divide life between them.'

The house still known as Lynch's Castle, although the most perfect example now remaining, was at one period by no means a solitary instance of the decorated habitations of the Galway merchants. The name of Lynch, as either provost, portreve, sovereign, or mayor of Galway, occurs no fewer than ninety-four times between the years 1274 and 1654; after that year it does not appear once. The house here pictured was the residence of the family for many generations. It had, however, several branches, whose

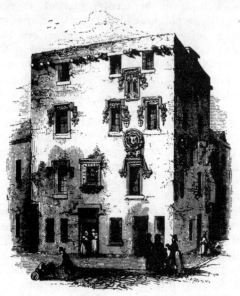

LYNCH'S CASTLE

habitations are frequently pointed out by their armorial bearings, or their crest, a lynx, over the gateway. One of its members is famous in history as the Irish Junius Brutus. The mere fact is sufficiently wonderful without the aid of invention; but it has, as may be supposed, supplied materials to a host of romancers. The story is briefly this:

James Lynch Fitzstephen was mayor or warden of Galway in 1493; he traded largely with Spain, and sent his son on a voyage thither to purchase and bring back a cargo of wine. Young Lynch, however, spent the money entrusted to him, and obtained credit from the Spaniard, whose nephew accompanied the youth back to Ireland to be paid the debt and establish further intercourse. The ship proceeded on her homeward voyage, and as she drew near the Irish shore, young Lynch conceived the idea of concealing his crime by committing another. Having seduced or frightened the crew into becoming participators, the youth was seized and thrown overboard. The father and friends of Lynch received the voyager with joy; and the murderer in a short time became himself a prosperous merchant. Security had lulled every sense of danger, and he proposed for a very beautiful girl, the daughter of a wealthy neighbour, in marriage. The proposal was accepted; but previous to the appointed day, one of the seamen became suddenly ill, and in a fit of remorse summoned old Lynch to the dying-bed, and communicated to him a full relation of the villany of his only and beloved son. Young Lynch was tried, found guilty, and sentenced to execution—the father being his judge. The wretched prisoner, however, had many friends among the people, and his relatives resolved with them that he should not die a shameful death. They determined upon his rescue. We copy the last act of the tragedy from Hardiman's *History of Galway*. 'Day had scarcely broken when the signal of preparation was heard among the guards without. The father rose, and assisted the executioner to remove the fetters which bound his unfortunate son. Then unlocking the door, he placed him between the priest and himself, leaning upon an arm of each. In this manner they ascended a flight of steps lined with soldiers, and were passing on to gain the street, when a new trial assailed the magistrate, for which he appears not to have been unprepared. His wretched wife, whose name was Blake, failing in her personal exertions to save the life of her son, had gone in distraction to the heads of her own family, and prevailed on them, for the honour of their house, to rescue him from ignominy. They flew to arms, and a prodigious concourse soon assembled to support them, whose outcries for mercy to the culprit would have shaken any nerves less firm than those of the mayor of Galway. He exhorted them to yield submission to the laws of their country; but finding all his efforts fruitless to accomplish the ends of justice at the accustomed place, and by the usual hands, he, by a desperate victory over parental feeling, resolved himself to perform the sacrifice which he had vowed to pay on its altar. Still retaining a hold of his unfortunate son, he mounted with him by a winding stair within the building, that led to an arched window overlooking the street, which he saw filled with the populace. Here he secured the end of the rope—which had been previously fixed round the neck of his son—to an iron staple, which projected from the wall, and after taking from him a last embrace, he launched him into eternity. The intrepid magistrate expected instant death from the fury of the populace; but the people seemed so much overawed or confounded by the magnanimous act, that they retired slowly and peaceably to their several dwellings. The innocent cause of this sad tragedy is said to have died soon after of grief, and the unhappy father of Walter Lynch to have secluded himself during the remainder of his life from all society except that of his mourning family. His house still exists in Lombard Street, Galway, which is yet known by the name of 'Dead Man's Lane'; and over the front doorway are to be seen a skull and crossbones executed in black marble, with the motto, "Remember Deathe—vaniti of vaniti, and all is but vaniti'".

The house in which the tragedy is said to have occurred was taken down only so recently as 1849; but the tablet which contains the skull and cross-bones bears the date 1624—upwards of a century after the alleged date of the occurrence.

37. THE MAID OF BALLYHAUNIS

My Mary dear! for thee I die
  O! place thy hand in mine, love—
My fathers here were chieftains high,
  Then to my plaints incline, love.
O, Plaited-hair! that now we were
  In wedlock's band united,

For, maiden mine, in grief I'll pine,
    Until our vows are plighted!

Thou, Rowan-bloom, since thus I rove,
    All worn and faint to greet thee,
Come to these arms, my constant love,
    With love as true to meet me!
Alas! my head—its wits are fled,
    I've failed in filial duty—
My sire did say, 'Shun, shun, for aye
    That Ballyhaunis beauty!'

But thy *Cúilin bán* I mark'd one day,
    Where the blooms of the bean-field cluster,
Thy bosom white like ocean's spray,
    Thy cheek like rowan-fruit's lustre,
Thy tones that shame the wild birds' fame
    Which sing in the summer weather—
And O! I sigh that thou, love, and I
    Steal not from this world together!

If with thy lover thou depart
    To the Land of Ships, my fair love,
No weary pain of head or heart,
    Shall haunt our slumbers there, love—
O! haste away, ere cold death's prey,
    My soul from thee withdrawn is;
And my hope's reward, the churchyard sward,
    In the town of Ballyhaunis!

38. NEVER THE TWAIN SHALL MEET

The 1840 canal built to link Lough Corrib and Lough Mask
was constructed on porous limestone so that when it was
filled the water soon seeped away. Engineers had the bright
idea of pouring in a clay bed. This was done but a second
trial showed that one of the lakes was higher than the other
and the project was abandoned leaving a quay that was
never used and a bridge under which no water ever flowed.

The designer was an Englishman.

39. WESTPORT TOWN

Farewell to Old Ireland, it is my native ground,
To my friends and neighbours near Westport town;
It was there I was reared from my infancy,
And in search of promotion I am going to sea,
When I think of going, my heart it does bleed
To think of my darling, but since it is decreed,
And to think how I spent the winter night round,
Along with lovely Mary of sweet Westport town.

When my foot is on the ocean, my heart is on dry land,
With a troubled mind on the deck I will stand,
When I gaze all around me the tears will fall down,
When I think of lovely Mary of sweet Westport town.
It is straight to America we are bound to steer;
Unto Philadelphia of fame and renown,
Where there, I intend my fortune to gain,
In hopes to return to sweet Westport again.

From Dublin's sweet city we mean to set sail,
Kind Providence protect us with a pleasant gale,
In company with Irishmen the glass will go round,
Here's a health to lovely Mary of Westport town.
It is not for riches that I love my dear,
But was I a lord of ten thousand pounds a year,
Or, had I the wealth of great Marquis Brown,
I would resign it lovely Mary of sweet Westport town.

40. THE BLACK CHAFER

It was a tramp from the Joyce country who came into our
house one wild wintry night that told us the story of the
'Black Chafer' as we sat around the fire.

The wind was wailing around the house, like women
keening the dead, as he was speaking, and he made his
voice rise or fall according as the wind rose or fell.

He was a tall man with wild eyes and his clothes were

almost in tatters. In a way, I was afraid of him, when I first saw him, and his story did nothing to lessen that fear.

'The three most blessed animals in the world,' he said, 'are the haddock, the robin and the lady-bird. And the three most cursed animals are the snake, the wren and the black chafer. And the black chafer is the most cursed of them all.

'I know that only too well. If a man should kill your son, woman of the house, never call him a black chafer, or if a woman should come between you and your husband, don't compare her with the black chafer.'

'God save us,' my mother said.

'Amen,' he replied.

The tramp didn't speak again for some time. We all stayed quiet because we knew he was going to tell us a story. It wasn't long before he began.

When I was a boy (he began), there was a woman in our village that everyone was afraid of. She lived in a little lonely cabin in a mountain-gap and nobody would ever go near her house. Neither would she come near anyone's house herself. Nobody would speak to her when they met her on the road, and she never stopped to talk with anybody either.

You would have pity for the creature just to see her walking the roads by herself, alone.

'Who is she,' I used to ask my mother, 'or why won't they speak to her?'

'Shh-hh- boy,' she always replied. 'That's the Black Chafer, a woman with a curse on her.'

'What did she do or who put the curse on her?'

'She was cursed by a priest, they say, but nobody knows what she did.'

And that's all the information I could get about her until I was a grown chap. Even then, I could find out nothing, except that she committed some dreadful sin, when she was young, and that she was cursed publicly by a priest on account of it. One Sunday, when the people were assembled at Mass, the priest turned around and said from the altar:

'There is a woman here that will merit eternal damnation for herself and for every person friendly with her. And I say to

61

that woman, that she is a cursed woman, and I say to you, to be as neighbourly to her, as you would be to a black chafer.'

'Then he said: "Rise up now, Black Chafer, and avoid the company of decent people from this out!"'

The poor woman got up and went out of the chapel. She was never called anything after that, except The Black Chafer, and her real name was soon forgotten. It was said that she had the evil eye. If she ever looked on a calf or sheep that wasn't her own, the animals died. Before long, the women were afraid to let their children out on the village street if she was passing by.

I married a very attractive girl when I was twenty-one. We had a little girl and were expecting another child. One day when I was cutting turf on the bog, my wife was feeding the hens in the street, when she saw — God between us and harm — the Black Chafer coming up the bohereen carrying the girl in her arms. One of the child's arms was woven around the woman's neck, and her shawl covered the mite's little body. My wife was speechless!

The Black Chafer laid the little girl in her mother's arms and my wife noticed that her clothes were wet.

'What happened the child?' she asked.

'She was looking for water-lilies around the Pool of the Rushes when she fell in,' the woman replied. 'I was crossing the road when I heard her screaming. I jumped over the ditch and managed to catch her just in the nick of time.'

'May God reward you,' said my wife. The other woman went off before she had time to say anymore. My wife brought the child inside, dried her and put her to bed. When I came home from the bog she told me what had happened. We both prayed for the Black Chafer that night.

The following day, the little girl began to prattle about the woman that saved her. 'The water was in my mouth, and in my eyes and in my ears,' she told us, 'I saw shining sparks and heard a great noise; I was slipping and slipping and suddenly I felt a hand about me, and she lifted me up and kissed me. I thought I was at home when I was in her arms with her shawl around me.'

A few days after that, my wife discovered that the child

was missing. She was missing for a couple of hours. When she came home, she told us that she was after paying a visit to the woman that saved her life. 'She made a cake for me,' she told us. 'There is nobody in the house but herself so I promised her that I'd call in to see her every day.'

Neither my wife nor I could say a word against her. The Black Chafer was after saving the girl's life so it wouldn't have been natural to prevent her from going up to the lonely house in the gap of the mountain. From that day onwards the child went up the hill to see her every evening.

The neighbours told us that it wasn't right. In a way, we knew that we were wrong, but how could we help it?

Would you believe me, friends? From the day the Black Chafer laid eyes on the little girl she began to dwindle and dwindle like a fire that couldn't be kindled! She soon lost her appetite and strength and after three months she was only a shadow. A month later she was in the churchyard.

The Black Chafer came down the mountain the day she was buried. They wouldn't let her into the graveyard. She turned back sorrowfully and slowly traced her footsteps up the mountain path again. I pitied the poor creature, because I knew that our trouble was no heavier than her own.

The next morning I went up the mountain path myself. I meant to tell her that neither my wife nor myself bore her any grudge or blamed her for what had happened. I knocked at her door but got no answer. I went in and saw that the ashes were red on the hearth. There was nobody at all to be seen. Then I noticed a bed in a corner of the room, so I went over to it. The Black Chafer was lying on it. . . cold and dead.

From that day onwards my household and myself have been plagued with disaster. My wife died in childbirth a month afterwards. The baby didn't survive. My cattle picked up some disease the following winter and the landlord put me out of my holding. I have been travelling the roads of Connacht, as a walking man, ever since.

Draw near true lovers and pay attention,
All that ever felt Cupid's dart,
I'm captivated and ruinated.
By a young female that won my heart.
My mind's tormented I can't prevent it.
Her glancing beauty has me destroyed,
I speak sincerely, I love her dearly.
She's lovely Mary of the Shannon side.

In the month of May when lambkins play.
By the river's side as I chanced to rove,
It's here I spied Mary both tight and airy,
Singing sweetly thro'the silent grove.
I got enchanted I sobbed and panted,
Like one distracted I stood and cried.
Ah! lovely creature, the pride of nature
Did Cupid send you to the Shannon side.

She then made answer, it's all romancing
For you to flatter a simple dame,
I'm not so stupid or duped by Cupid,
So I defy you on me to scheme,
My habitation's near this plantation,
I feed my flocks by the river side.
Therefore don't tease me and you'd please me
Said lovely Mary of the Shannon side.

I say, my charmer, my soul's alarmer,
Your glancing beauty did me ensnare,
If I offended I ne'er intended,
To hurt your feelings I declare.
You sang so sweetly and so discreetly,
You cheered the woods and valleys wide,
The great Apollo your voice would follow,
Should he but hear you near the Shannon side.

Young man you're dreaming or you are scheming
You're like the serpent that tempted Eve,
Your oily speeches do sting like leeches,
But all your flattery shall not me deceive,
Your vain delusion is an intrusion,
For your misconduct I do you chide,
Therefore retire, it is my desire,
Said lovely Mary of the Shannon side.

Don't be so cruel, my dearest jewel,
I'm captivated I really am
To show I'm loyal, make no denial,
Here is my hand and I'll wed you now,
I want no sporting nor deadly courting,
But instantly I'll make you my bride,
Therefore surrender, I'm no pretender,
Sweet lovely maid of the Shannon side.

Unto the Chapel we went straight way,
We quickly hurried and both got married,
And joined our hearts on that very day,
Her parents blessed and then caressed us
A handsome portion they did us provide,
They may bless the day I chanced to stray
By the lovely banks of the Shannon side,
By the lovely banks of the Shannon side.

42. LIGHT AND DARKNESS

In the villages clustering among the foothills surrounding
the base of Croagh Patrick, and on the plains spreading out
towards the west, many a wonderful tale is still related and
numerous are the folk-stories told in the soft, warm glow of
the turf-fires during the long winter evenings. Balor, of the
Evil-Eye, is still remembered, and the exploits of Finn and
his Fianna are to this day recounted by the old people; and
though the young, learned in the culture of the National
School, profess to scoff at wondertales while the noon-day

sun glows overhead, they go in fear and trembling in the night time over ground rendered sacred by hero exploit and the old people's unquestioned belief. A glorious land this west land of ours. The mighty Croagh looks down on all the world-changes. It has seen the hoary head of Druid Priest bending low in worship as the sungod leaped into the heavens. It has witnessed the countless thousands swarming round its base when our great forefathers, before Lugnasa, gathered to worship Crom, the beneficient All-Giver. In Christian times it witnessed the self-same pilgrimage a living force, but now undertaken in honour of the God of Gods.

Away on the southern side of this mountain, today, stretch leagues of barren upland, interspersed with occasional patches laboriously fertilised. Quite different the aspect hundreds of years before Christian man trod on Irish soil. Then over all this land of poverty and desolation stretched vast woodlands with many a pleasant, fertile and cultivated place between, and river and lake teeming with fish. Truly a land overflowing with milk and honey. He who digs for turf today discloses roots of huge trees, oak and fir and birch, and now and again the interwoven wattle with which our forefathers builded to themselves an habitation durable and warm.

In those dim and misty ages of Erin's glory all this land was wasted by the ravages of a fierce, wicked and mighty Boar. To the west and the south of the Croagh his sway extended, and those who were of the soil went forth in fear and trembling, unknowing the time when the lord of the district would demand of them a tribute fated with life and substance. The favourite house of this tyrant was on the cliff over-hanging Lougheen Alla. To the southern slopes of Croagh, one bright morning in springtime, there came two Princesses of Light, accompanied by noble hounds, intent upon rousing from his lair and ridding the earth of this black tyrant and his brood, whose devastating rule made of this fair countryside a land wanting the good God's blessing. They were daughters of the King. Both were famed as huntresses, tall and fair and stately. Like melted and running gold the hairs on their heads. Their garments interwoven with findruiney and above the rainbow in the beauty and number of the ever-changing colours. Crossing the shallow and angry Avon Buidhe, the Princesses soon drew near to the den of the great Black Pig. Fiercely rousing himself, the cruel all-slaying lord of the pigs stood forth on the cliff beside his dwelling. His tusks were round as a hero's shield, glittering like silver in the light of the morning's sun. His eyes gave forth the fire of fierce anger, the hair on his back and neck standing erect like to the bristles of the hedge-hog. Loud rang the challenge, and louder rings the answering cry when the huntress-princesses loosed their noble hounds. High swelled the din of conflict as the champions of Light in many a fierce encounter forced the Lord of Darkness from his stronghold. Back, always backwards, he was driven. The bright face of Aidan Bannis splashed red with blood of many a champion. Blood-red is the colour it throws back to the kiss of the noon-day sun. Down into the hazel woods of Boris, where many a fired and pointed stake protects the villages in their pleasant clearings. The Pig fights hard in defence of his clan, but today no pointed stake, no hero feint avails. Louder and fiercer rings the cry of conflict as interwoven pallisade goes down and wattled dun is given to the fire faggot. Swelling back from the foothills of Croagh come warrior frenzy. And the sea moaning round all of Lachta and Cregan Roe, which received its name on that day. The fierce, vehement shouts were borne outward terror laden on the wings of the wind to the ever restless sea. Great fear and dismay seized on the Druid Priests of Caher's Holy Island when the fierce hero shouts were borne out to them in the lap of the wind, and they lifted up their voices in supplication to the throne of their God, beseeching protection from warrior frenzy. And the sea moaned round all the islands in sympathy.

Throughout the day the fierce stubborn fight on land continues. The Black Pig struggles valiantly, though driven from one stronghold to another. Towards the close of the day the pursuit still continuing—the Princesses, with two of their favourite and noblest hounds, always pressing close the chase—the Black Boar, followed by what remained of his followers, rushed towards a small lake and with a loud resounding roar, disappeared beneath the hissing waters in a blaze of flame, followed closely by the two hounds, all vanishing from mortal view together.

Even to the present day peasants on their way home at night time have seen the glitter of fierce eyes shining like balls of fire out of the surrounding darkness and to some is given the knowledge of a huge Pig feeding close to the shores of the lake, and the country people tell strange tales of wild pigs that at night time come out to graze on the shores of Lough na Muca, and of the cry of gallant hounds, and of wild midnight hunts, and of beautiful shadowy princesses and of the grief of the princesses who for ever wail the fate of noble hounds on the shores of Lough na Bainne Rioghan.

43. MY OWN MAYO

There's a green glen nestles far from the city's ways,
Where the birds are ever songful how-so dark the days;
Where a laughing river's voice chases sorrowing and woe
From the changing heart of man, in my own Mayo!

Oh! the spring her fairest blooms to the branches brings,
And the thrush her sweetest tunes in their shelter sings;
And the woodbine-scented breeze murmurs musical and low
Through that glad and grassy glen in my own Mayo.

Long and often have I laid where the grass grows high,
And listened to the stream as it warbled by,
And thought that earth held naught that could thrill me so
As the music of that river in my own Mayo!

But a sweeter sound I've heard, and blooms more bright
Than the spring brings in her train have cheered my sight;
And a light has lit my heart with a nameless glow,
In that lone and lovely valley in my own Mayo!

Bud and blossoms, breeze and river, might with distance
    pale,
But that light and voice shall ever over Time prevail;
At its whisper flies the present and my thoughts all go
To a girl in that valley in my own Mayo!

Oh! the city's glare awhile may joy and mirth impart,
But can ne'er unloose the tendrils that entwine the heart,
And bring back some gleam of sunshine from long ago
That recalls what binds me ever to my own Mayo!

44. CONNAMARA

Oughterarde is termed the entrance to Connamara, but the
boundaries seem somewhat undefined, like the sensations
induced by wildly beautiful scenery.

> The vague emotion of delight
> While climbing up some Alpine height.

Measured and mapped Connamara may be, but painted or
described it never can. Those sublime landscapes of mountain, moor, and mire, are photographed on the memory for
ever, but cannot be reproduced on canvas; and a great
master of art, a Michael Angelo (Titmarsh) throws down
his brush, with the wise confession, 'All that we can do is to
cry, Beautiful!' Who shall take it up and paint? Not mine, a
prentice hand, to daub a caricature (about as like the
original, as a pastile to Vesuvius, or a 'cinder-tip' to the
Himalayas) of those glorious Irish Alps, of the Maum-Turk
mountains, or of Bina Beola, rising, in solemn majesty,
amid a sea of golden and roseate flowers. It requires a con-
fidence which I do not feel, to attempt the Hallelujah
Chorus on my penny trumpet, or, where Phidias distrusts
his chisel, to commence a Colossus with my knife and fork.
But I shall never forget our silent happiness, a happiness
like childhood's, so complete and pure, as, mile after mile,
we watched the sunlight and the shadows, sweeping over
the hill, and lake, and plain, (so swiftly that every minute

the whole view seemed to change), and saw the snow-white
goats among the purple heath, and the kine, jet-black and
glowing red, knee-deep in the silver waters.

45. A MASSACRE

You Roman Catholics I pray draw near,
Some dismal verses you now shall hear,
It is concerning a most brutal deed,
That would make the hardest heart to bleed,

Upon the 21st day of July,
Those fine young youths were compell'd to die,
In Six-mile-bridge in the County Clare,
To see the elections was what brought them there.

About twelve that day as we have been told,
The streets were crowded with both young and old
When the 31st were marching by that way,
But there one officer made them delay.

Then like wolves, blood thirsty, that lost their prey
Those vile assassins without delay,
Commenced to fire the Cromwellian core,
And left many weltering all in their gore.

Then most heart-rending it was to see,
So many murdered innocently,
By those cruel barbarians without fear or dread
Fathers, sons and brothers they were shot dead.

The Rev. Father Clune was wounded sore,
That blessed divine they left him in his gore,
Amongst the dead and dying he was seen to fall
For they grazed his temple with a musket ball.

Such a dreadful carnage was never knew,
As was committed by the wick'd crew —

70

When they shot the father they then began
With their bayonets fixed to guillotine the son!

It would draw tears then down from your eyes
To hear the widows and the orphan's cries
Likewise the mother for her son insane,
Each seeking out their own amongst the slain.

Now the friends and parents of the murder'd dead
May weep and mourn o'er their grassy bed —
And in night's dead silence offer up their prayers
For the innocent victims of the County Clare.

That cruel and cold-blooded Massacre,
Of Six-mile-bridge will remembered be,
Where young and old that day lost their life
By a most infernal barbarian tribe.

Now let each good Christian with hearts sincere
To the Almighty offer up their prayers,
That their souls in heaven may happy be,
To the end of time and eternity.

46. PRISON REFORMS

. . . It appears by a record of the reign of Edward I that in
1303, there was no public prison in Connaught; but this
defect was soon after remedied. On the division of the pro-
vince into counties in 1585, the gaol of the newly-created
County of Galway was established in the central town of
Loughrea. Here it continued until 1674, when it was reported to be 'so old and ruinous' that the judge of the assize
recommended the grand jury to build a new gaol in the
town of Galway and in the meantime directed that the
prisoners should be taken care of. They were accordingly
brought to Galway and lodged in the town gaol, which was
made use of by the county sheriffs until 1686 when a strong
castle situated near the west bridge, and adjoining the town

walls was selected by the grand jury to serve as a gaol for the county.

In 1788 Mr Howard visited the prison, of which he gave the following account: Galway county gaol is near the river; there is a new court but no pump; the criminals are in two long rooms with dirt floors and no fire-place; the debtors have small rooms above the stairs. Allowance to felons, a sixpenny loaf of household bread every other day, (weight three pound twelve ounces) which they often sell for four pence halfpenny to buy potatoes. Gaolers' salary 20/- 1788 April 1. Debtors 4. Felons etc. 14.

47. NICE LITTLE JANE FROM BALLINASLOE

You lads that are funny, and call maids your honey,
   Give ear for a moment, I'll not keep you long.
I'm wounded by Cupid, he has made me stupid,
   To tell you the truth now, my brain's nearly wrong;
A neat little posy, who does live quite cosy,
   Has kept me unable to walk to and fro;
Each day I'm declining, in love I'm repining,
   For nice little Jenny from Ballinasloe.

It was in September, I'll ever remember,
   I went out to walk by a clear river side
For sweet recreation, but, to my vexation,
   This wonder of Nature I quickly espied;
I stood for to view her an hour I'm sure;
   The earth could not show such a damsel, I know,
As that little girl, the pride of the world,
   Called nice little Jenny from Ballinasloe.

I said to her: 'Darling! this is a nice morning;
   The birds sing enchanting, which charms the groves;
Their notes do delight me, and you do invite me,
   Along this clear water some time for to rove.
Your beauty has won me and surely undone me;
   If you won't agree for to cure my sad woe,

So great is my sorrow, I'll ne'er see tomorrow,
    My sweet little Jenny from Ballinasloe.'

'Sir, I did not invite you, nor yet dare not slight you;
    You're at your own option to act as you please;
I am not ambitious, nor e'er was officious,
    I am never inclined to disdain or to tease;
I love conversation, likewise recreation,
    I'm free with a friend, and I'm cold with a foe;
But virtue's my glory, and will be till I'm hoary,'
    Said nice little Jenny from Ballinasloe.

'Most lovely of creatures! your beautiful features
    Have sorely attracted and captured my heart;
If you won't relieve me, in truth you may believe me,
    Bewildered in sorrow till death I must smart;
I'm at your election, so grant me protection,
    And feel for a creature that's tortured in woe;
One smile it will heal me; one frown it will kill me;
Sweet nice little Jenny from Ballinasloe!'

'Sir, yonder's my lover, if he should discover
    Or ever take notice you spoke unto me,
He'd close your existence in spite of resistance;
    Be pleased to withdraw, then, lest he might you see:
You see he's approaching, then don't be encroaching,
    He has his large dog and his gun there also;
Although you're a stranger I wish you from danger,'
    Said nice little Jenny from Ballinasloe.

I bowed then genteely, and thanked her quite freely;
    I bid her adieu and took to the road;
So great was my trouble my pace I did double;
    My heart was oppressed and sank down with the load.
For ever I'll mourn for beauteous Jane Curran,
    And ramble about in affection and woe,
And think on the hour I saw that sweet flower,
    My dear little Jenny from Ballinasloe!

48. PARNELLITE PUBLIC OPINION

We have had some curious manifestations during the last few days of the value that should be attached to Parnellite public opinion. Certain writers in the Factionist Press are constantly asserting that Dublin is Ireland — that when the voice of Dublin is heard, Ireland speaks. They claim it as the one great centre of independent thought, where everything is mighty and great and all things provincial are petty and contemptible. . .

49. DAVITT

In 1846, the year that Parnell was born, Michael Davitt too saw the light of day. His youth was influenced by James Fintan Lalor and he believed that the abolition of the existing landlord-tenant structure was necessary not alone for the dignity of the peasantry but for the good of society as a whole. Davitt's own family had been evicted from its small Mayo farmhouse and the child Michael went to work early at a Lancashire mill. His arm was severed in an accident at the mill when he was but eleven years of age.

He grew up with a thirst for knowledge of his native land. He was arrested in 1870 for arms trafficking on behalf of the Irish Republican Brotherhood.

In 1878 he met John Devoy in America, where he was lecturing. From abroad he exhorted the Irish to seek public office and pursue every reform possible which might lead to independence. A type of co-partnership between landlord and tenant was one of the things he had in mind. Devoy, on the other hand, favoured the complete abolition of landlordism.

Believing that the strong Irish preoccupation with land would prosper in a nationalisation of land rather than its ownership that then seemed so impractical, Davitt founded the Irish National Land League, a movement that has existed in various forms since that time.

Michael Davitt was born in Strade, near Bellavary. He died in 1906.

50. THE PLAYBOY

PEGEEN: *(Looking at him playfully)* And it's that kind of a poacher's love you'd make, Christy Mahon, on the sides of Neifin, when the night is down?

CHRISTY: It's little you'll think if my love's a poacher's, or an earl's itself, when you'll feel my two hands stretched around you, and I squeezing kisses on your puckered lips, till I'd feel a kind of pity for the Lord God is all ages sitting lonesome in His golden chair.

PEGEEN: That'll be right fun, Christy Mahon, and any girl would walk her heart out before she'd meet a young man was your like for eloquence, or talk at all.

CHRISTY: *(Encouraged)* Let you wait to hear me talking till we're astray in Erris, when Good Friday's by, drinking a sup from a well, and making mighty kisses with our wetted mouths, or gaming in a gap of sunshine, with yourself stretched back unto your necklace, in the flowers of the earth.

PEGEEN: *(In a low voice, moved by his tone)* I'd be nice so, is it?

CHRISTY: *(With rapture)* If the mitred bishops seen you that time, they'd be the like of the holy prophets, I'm thinking, do be straining the bars of paradise to lay eyes on the Lady Helen of Troy, and she abroad, pacing back and forward, with a nosegay in her golden shawl.

PEGEEN: *(With real tenderness)* And what is it I have, Christy Mahon, to make me fitting entertainment for the like of you, that has such poet's talking, and such bravery of heart.

CHRISTY: *(In a low voice)* Isn't there the light of seven heavens in your heart alone, the way you'll be an angel's lamp to me from this out, and I abroad in the darkness, spearing salmons in the Owen or the Carromore?

PEGEEN: If I was your wife I'd be along with you those nights, Christy Mahon, the way you'd see I was a great hand at coaxing bailiffs, or coining funny nicknames for the stars of night.

CHRISTY: You is it? Taking your death in the hailstones, or

in the fogs of dawn.

PEGEEN: Yourself and me would shelter easy in a narrow bush *(with a qualm of dread)*; but we're only talking, maybe, for this would be a poor, thatched place to hold a fine lad the like of you.

CHRISTY: *(Putting his arm round her)* If I wasn't a good Christian, it's on my naked knees I'd be saying my prayers and paters to every jackstraw you have roofing your head, and every stony pebble is paving the laneway to your door.

PEGEEN: *(Radiantly)* If that's the truth I'll be burning candles from this time out to the miracles of God that have brought you from the south today, and I with my gowns bought ready, the way I can wed you, and not wait at all.

CHRISTY: It's miracles, and that's the truth. Me there toiling a long while, and walking a long while, not knowing at all I was drawing all times nearer to this holy day.

PEGEEN: And myself, a girl, was tempted often to go sailing the seas till I'd marry a Jew-man, with ten kegs of gold, and I not knowing at all there was the like of you drawing nearer, like the stars of God.

CHRISTY: And to think I'm long years hearing women talking that talk, to all bloody fools, and this the first time I've heard the like of your voice talking sweetly for my own delight.

PEGEEN: And to think it's me is talking sweetly, Christy Mahon, and I the fright of seven townlands for my biting tongue. Well, the heart's a wonder; and I'm thinking, there won't be our like in Mayo, for gallant lovers, from this hour today.

51. O'RUARK'S SONG

The valley lay smiling before me,
   Where lately I left her behind;
Yet I trembled and something hung o'er me,
   That saddened the joy of my mind.

76

I looked for the lamp which, she told me,
  Should shine when her pilgrim returned;
But though darkness began to enfold me,
  No lamp from the battlements burned.

I flew to her chamber—'twas lonely,
  As if the lov'd tenant lay dead —
Ah! would it were death and death only!
  But no, the young false one had fled.
And there hung the lute that could soften
  My very worst pains into bliss,
While the hand that had waked it so often
  Now throbbed to a proud rival's kiss.

There *was* a time, falsest of women!
  When Breffni's good sword would have sought
That man, through a million of foemen
  Who dared but to wrong thee *in thought!*
While now—O degenerate daughter
  Of Erin, how fallen is thy fame!
And through ages of bondage and slaughter,
  Our country shall bleed for thy shame.

Already the curse is upon her
  And strangers her valleys profane;
They come to divide—to dishonour,
  And tyrants they long will remain.
But onward! — the green banner rearing,
  Go, flesh every sword to the hilt;
On *our* side is Virtue and Erin,
  On *theirs* is the Saxon and Guilt.

52. STRONGHOLD

Dromahair was the capital of Brefni O'Rourke. The
O'Rourkes had castles at Leitrim, Carrickallen and Castle-
car, but Dromahair was their chief stronghold. The ruins of
their castle stand on the outskirts of the little town,

beside a river, overlooking a valley. Both the castle and valley are famed in song and story. Moore's verses will occur to you as you stand in the ivy-clad ruins. You remember the lines of course:

> The valley lay smiling before me
> Where lately I left her behind;
> Yet I trembled and something hung o'er me,
> That saddened the joy of my mind.
> I look for the lamp which she told me
> Should shine when her pilgrim returned;
> Yet though darkness began to enfold me,
> No lamp from the battlements burned.

Well, here you have the valley that lay smiling before him. Here were also the battlements, now no more. They were battered to fragments in the wars of the sixteenth century, but some of the walls remain.

Here Dermod MacMurrough and Dervorgilla, the wife of Tiernan O'Rourke, used to meet. They finally bolted during the absence of O'Rourke, and hence the infamy that has lived on through the ages. When MacMurrough was obliged to fly the country from the vengeance of O'Rourke, he went to England and brought back the Normans. It was a terrible crime, a terrible wrong, a terrible atonement. MacMurrogh died, falling to pieces, in the pangs of a loathsome disease, and the evil he did lived after him.

53: THE LOVELY MAID OF THE SHANNON STREME

> As I walk'd out of a summer's morning
> It's unto Mohill I took my way,
> Where the valleys were deck'd with daisies
> And fruitful gardens in rich array.
> Where I espied a lovely fair one,
> Whose killing glances did me ensnare,
> While viewing her beauty I got quite stupid
> And to approach her I got afraid.

I then accosted this lovely fair one,
To tell her name and her dwelling place,
Or was she Hebe or lovely Seres,
Or Vulcan's bride whom the apple gain'd,
She then made answer I am no goddess,
I am no proud or immortal dame,
My appellation I must leave mysterious,
I live convenient to the Shannon stream.

She would read most neatly on cloth paper
The whole creation by land or sea,
The ships that's sailing upon the ocean,
The groves and gardens and meadows green
The moon and stars in their glittering motion
That rules the night till the break of day,
The brilliant Phoebus that crowns our labours
The wolf and tiger the buck and bear.

I then requested this lovely fair one,
To extricate me from grief and woe,
As I'm here condoling through love and nature
Since I have seen you mo mhíle stór
My youthful days they are passing over
And no consolement to be obtained,
But if I die through your means mo stóirín
I'll surely haunt you both night and day.

She says refrain from such persuasions,
Your introduction is all in vain
You're not as stupid as you pretend it,
To think to marry a poor servant maid,
I'd take my time till I meet my equals,
And that won't be till the Lord is pleased,
It's with His bounty he feeds the ravens,
I'll live in hopes and I'll ne'er despair.

I being quite languid my limbs grew weary
I supplicated this lovely dame,
For to tie my head and show some nature,

And I would place her free from being a slave
She then consented to cure my ailments
Our joys were greater than I could relate,
I made her mistress of all my holdings
Hard by sweet Mohill that lovely place.

54. PADRAIG'S PENCE

O Padraig dear and did you hear the boys are coming
    round,
And the girls too to ask of you a penny or a pound
To help to spread the Irish speech again from shore to
    shore
And make our land as strong and grand as in the days of
    yore.
O, I met Sean T. Ó Ceallaigh, and he took me by the hand,
And says he, 'I want brave lads like you to tramp through-
    out the land.
Every day and night of Language Week, and never know
    fatigue
Till you have gathered pence and pounds to help the Gaelic
    League.'

'We're fighting many a foe,' says he, 'At home and far away
With every English understrapper blocking up our way;
We're fighting for the life of Ireland, shrined within her
    speech —
The speech that Colm Cille and Ciaran showed us how to
    teach;
And we'll win,' says he, 'but every fighter needs a helping
    hand,
And money is our need today against the grabber band.
We'll beat their schemers and their knaves, their force and
    their intrigue,
If Ireland fills the War Chest of the dauntless Gaelic
    League.'

55. POOKA PIPES

Croagh Patrick, a mountain overlooking Clew Bay is a famous place of penance. A pooka once took a half-fool of a piper from Dunmore in the County Galway to a big feast in the house of the Banshee atop the mountain. The piper was pleased enough because it would save him doing the penance he had received for stealing the priest's gander. In the palace was a well laid out table but the ladies sitting around it were ugly *cailleacha*. The pooka bid the piper play for the company and the sweetest music ever heard came from the pipes. The women paid gold and the Dunmore man began to think he was on to a good thing when from an adjoining room there flew the gander he had stolen — this despite the fact that the piper and his mother had eaten it.

The gander swept all the food off the table and was also waiting for the piper when he went outside to return home. He gave the piper a new set of pipes, which pleased him greatly. The pooka left the half-fool to Dunmore and on parting told him 'You have two things now that you never had before — sense and music'.

That wasn't absolutely correct for the new pipes given to him by the gander played a sound like all the ganders in Ireland were screeching. But like all good tales, the old pipes turned up and the half-fool played beautiful music on them. Some say, indeed, that he was the finest piper the west of Ireland ever had.

56. THE SPORTING RACES OF GALWAY

As I roved down to Galway town one day for recreation,
On the merry month of August as my mind was elevated
There were multitudes assembled with their tickets at the
       station,
That my eyes began to dazzle and they going to the races.

There were passengers from Limerick and passengers
     from Nenagh,

And passengers from Dublin and sportsmen from
        Tipperary,
There were passengers from Kerry where Dan was
        educated,
And the bold Clare Milesians who had gained
        emancipation.

There were multitudes from Aran though surrounded by
        the sea there
The boys from Connemara Ballyvaughan and Newquay
        there
There were people from all quarters of our little fertile
        nation
With the shout of 'home rule for Irishmen' that sprung
        convocation.

There were jaunting cars and carriages going to and fro like
        blazes,
And side cars back and forward there for very little wages
The steamers and the ferry boats well rigged for navigation,
And they ploughing the raging ocean to come and see the
        races.

The tents are in rotation in the middle of the races,
The stand house situated on a handsome elevation,
There were brandy, wine, and cordial with the best
        accommodation,
With a drop of potheen whisky that got no adulteration.

It's there you'd see confectioners with sugar sticks and
        dainties,
The lozenges and oranges the lemons and the raisins
The gingerbread and spices to accommodate the ladies,
And a pig's crubeen for three pence to be picking while
        your able.

It's there you'd see the gamblers the thimble men and
        garter,
The sporting wheel of fortune with four and twenty
        quarters,

And others without scruple pelting wattles at poor **Maggie**,
And her father well contented and he looking on his
     daughter.

It's there you see the pipers and fiddlers comparing
And the nimble footed dancers and the tripping on the
     daisies.
And others crying cigars and lights and bills of the races,
With the colour of the jockeys the prize and horses ages.

It's there you'd see the jockeys and they mounted up most
     stately,
With the orange and blue the red and green the emblem of
     the nation
When the bell was rung for starting the horses were
     impatient,
That you'd think th'ed ne'er set foot on ground the speed
     was so amazing.

The sporting boys of Paddy's land and Garryowen na
     gloria,
Our men stood up most manfully when tyrants did oppose
     him,
With the banner of his country the green across his
     shoulders,
The band played up in Germany the cause o're in the
     clover.

There was half a million of people there of all
     denominations,
The Protestants and candlesticks, the Jews and
     Presbyterians,
There was yet no animosity no matter what persuasion,
But peace and hospitality including fresh acquaintance.

So now my song is ended and my pen is out of order,
Success attend those Gentlemen who carry on the races,
May peace and true tranquillity abound throughout our
     nation,
And trade and commerce flourish as it was in former ages.

57. THE BIGGER THE BETTER

Ballinamore is a small town, existing, and existing very badly, by agriculture. The whole of the neighbourhood, with very few exceptions, is fearfully rack-rented: the land, which is generally poor, is let by competition to the highest bidder; and rents are covenanted for, that can never be paid. The property of Lord Southwell, however, which is situated in this district, is an exception. It is unquestionably amongst the nobility, and the largest proprietors, that these exceptions are chiefly to be found — a fact that may probably be attributable to the better circumstances of the great proprietors, who are not, generally, so embarrassed as the small landowners. I found that the landholders in the neighbourhood of Ballinamore were necessitated to send every particle of produce, except potatoes, to market, to make up their rents, and that they lived as miserably as the owner of the poorest cabin.

58. WESTERN HOLIDAY

The Midland Great Western's doing its best,
    And the circular ticket is safe in my vest;
But I feel that my holiday never begins
    Till I'm in Connemara among the Twelve Pins.

The bank has no fortune of mine to invest
    But there's money enough for the ones I love best;
All the gold that I want I shall find on the whins
    When I'm in Connemara among the Twelve Pins.

Down by the lough I shall wander once more,
    Where the wavelets lap lap round the stones on the shore;
And the mountainy goats will be wagging their chins
    As they pull at the bracken among the Twelve Pins.

And it's welcome I'll be, for no longer I'll meet,
    The hard, pallid faces I find in the street;

The girl with blue eyes, and the boy with brown shins,
  Will stand for their pictures among the Twelve Pins.

Tonight, when all London's with gaslight agleam,
  And the Carlton is filled with Society's cream,
I'll be 'takin' me tay' down at ould Johnny Flinn's
  Safe an' away in the heart o' the Pins.

59. LONG WALK

The great-granduncle of John D'Arcy (O'Dorsey) who
founded the town of Clifden in 1812 came from Kiltullagh,
near Athenry. A Jacobite, he became a brilliant scientist
and was a member of the French Academy. A story is told
about a tenant of his called Tomás.

While out walking one day Tomás met a stranger who
invited him to a wedding. He was reluctant to accept but
three more strangers appeared and prevailed on him to
accept the invitation. The R.S.V.P. was inclined to lose its
S.V.P. since it was made clear that acceptance was obliga-
tory!

The wedding was in Athlone and Tomás weakly suggest-
ed that he had not the strength to walk that far. In a field
nearby were four horses and the strangers indicated these.
Tomás became most considerate and insisted on walking
while the others rode the four horses. He was hoping to be
left so far behind that the wedding would be over before he
reached Athlone. He feared these men were out to kidnap
him for the ransom of a fine field of turnips he had ready for
harvesting.

They accepted the horses but they made Tomás ride a
calf that was in the field. Moreover they made him vow he
would not speak a word until they reached Athlone. Since
the calf was no Irish bull Tomás still hoped he would be left
trailing, especially when he arrived at the River Suck at
Ballinasloe. The river was sixty feet wide and twelve feet
deep.

A gallant little animal was this calf, however, and he

switched his tail, took a ram stam at the river and cleared it without getting a strand of his tail wet. In his admiration, Tomás forgot his compulsion to remain silent. 'Begad but there was never an animal to jump like that since Fionn's Bran was only two feet over a jamjar in height,' said he.

The strangers were angry at his disobedience and they rained blows upon him till he fell from his bovine mount. Tomás was lucky, however, for his speaking had broken their power over him. He awoke next morning on the banks of the Suck with only a little stiffness to remind him of his escapade. He walked back to Kiltullagh and noticed the four horses and the calf in the field again. He inquired if there had been a wedding in Athlone the previous day but found that there wasn't. Many months afterwards, however, he heard that music and singing had been heard from a *lios* at Baylough, near Athlone late on the same evening.

60. THE WEST CLARE RAILWAY

You may talk of Columbus's sailing
    Across the Atlantical sea
But he never tried to go railing
    From Ennis as far as Kilkee.
You run for the train in the mornin',
    The excursion train starting at eight,
You're there when the clock gives the warnin',
    And there for an hour you'll wait.

(Spoken): And as you're waiting in the train,
        You'll hear the guard sing this refrain:—

'Are ye right there, Michael? are ye right?
Do you think that we'll be there before the night?
    Ye've been so long in startin',
    That ye couldn't say for sartin' —
Still ye might now, Michael, so ye might!'

They find out where the engine's been hiding,
 And it drags you to Sweet Corofin;
Says the guard, 'Back her down on the siding
 There's the goods from Kilrush comin' in.'
Perhaps it comes in in two hours,
 Perhaps it breaks down on the way;
'If it does,' says the guard, 'be the powers
 We're here for the rest of the day!'

(Spoken): And while you sit and curse your luck,
    The train backs down into a truck.

'Are ye right there, Michael? are ye right?
Have ye got the parcel there for Mrs White?
  Ye haven't, Oh, Begorra,
  Say it's comin' down to-morra—
And it might now, Michael, so it might.'

At Lahinch the sea shines like a jewel,
 With joy you are ready to shout,
When the stoker cries out, 'There's no fuel,
 And the fire's taytotally out.
But hand up that bit of a log there—
 I'll soon have ye out of the fix;
There's a fine clamp of turf in the bog there';
 And the rest go a-gathering' sticks.

(Spoken): And while you're breakin' bits of trees,
    You hear some wise remarks like these:—

'Are ye right there, Michael? are ye right?
Do ye think ye can get the fire to light?
  Oh, an hour you'll require,
  For the turf it might be drier—
Well, it might now, Michael, so it might.'

Kilkee! Oh, you never get near it!
 You're in luck if the train brings you back,
For the permanent way is so queer, it

Spends most of its time off the track,
Uphill the ould engin' is climbin',
　While the passengers push with a will;
You're in luck when you reach Ennistymon,
　For all the way home is down-hill.

(Spoken):　And as you're wobbling through the dark,
　　　　　　　You hear the guard make this remark:—

'Are ye right there, Michael? are ye right?
Do you think that ye'll be home before it's light?'
　　''Tis all dependin' whether
　　　The ould engin' howlds together—'
'And it might now, Michael, so it might!'

61. HONOUR BEFORE LAND

A certain Clare landlord had the name of being in the
habit of inviting comely daughters of his tenants to
provide him with hospitality of a carnal nature at his
country house. Of a generous nature, however, he
also repaid their parents by increasing their holding.
Parents of particularly handsome daughters, therefore, ended up with good sized farms.

A visitor to the area many years afterwards could
not help noticing the small holding his aunt possessed
compared to her neighbours. He queried her on the
reason. Her answer was acid if accurate: 'Musha, son,
my grandmother never lifted her skirts above at the
big house.'

62. THE GIRL FROM CLARE

We were sittin' on the wall upon a Sunday
To watch the girls go by,
And thinkin' we'd be marrit to one one day
When Kate Flynn caught our eye,

88

Oh, man! she was the makin's of a fairy,
And it made each boyo swear,
'There's not one girl in the wide, wide world
Like the girl from the County Clare!

Chorus: And ev'ry man had got the finest plan
　　　　Ye ever see now—barrin' me now,
　　　　Ev'ry day there's one of them would say,
　　　　That she'll agree now—you'll see now;
　　　　All night they'd fight,
　　　　As to which o' them was right,
　　　　In the colour of her eyes and hair,
　　　　But not a word from me was ever heard,
　　　　About the darlin' girl from Clare!

Says Fagin,"'Tis the father I'll be plazin',
I'll tell him of the land I've tilled,
I'll tell him of the cattle I have grazin'
And the house I mean to build;
And whin he sees the 'arable' and 'pasture'
And the fat stock feedin' there,
An' the hens an' the chickens,
Ye may go to the dickens
For the girl from the County Clare.'

Chorus: So ev'ry man had got the finest plan
　　　　Ye ever see now—barrin' me now,
　　　　Ev'ry day there's one of them would say,
　　　　That she'll agree now—you'll see now;
　　　　Thinks I to meself
　　　　Though I haven't got the pelf,
　　　　Of brass I've got my share,
　　　　And so I know the way they ought to go
　　　　About the darlin' girl from Clare!

Sez Sharkey, 'She'll be coming to the shop there
To buy some sort of thing,
I'll ax her if she has a mind to stop there,
And should I buy the ring:

An' whin she sees the curtains on the windas,
An' the old clock on the stair
Keepin' time to the minit,
No one else will be in it
With the darlin' girl from Clare!'

Chorus: So ev'ry man had got the finest plan
Ye ever see now—barrin' me now,
Ev'ry day there's one of them would say,
That she'll agree now—you'll see now;
Thinks I,'Ye may stop,
Till yer dead in yer shop,
An' not a hair she'll care,
Wid all yer gold
Ye'll never hold a hold
Upon the darlin' girl from Clare!'

I never said a single word about her,
But I met the girl that day,
I told her I could never live widout her,
An' what had she to say?
She said that I might go and see her father:
I met him then and there,
An' in less than an hour
We were fightin' for the dower
Of the darlin' girl from Clare!

Chorus: So ev'ry man had got the finest plan
Ye ever see now—barrin' me now,
Ev'ry day there's one of them would say,
That she'll agree now—you'll see now;
But late last night
When the moon was bright
I axed her if she'd share
Me joy an' me sorra'—
An' begorra! on tomorra'
I'll be married to the girl from Clare!

63. KATHLEEN

The reaper's weary task was done,
And down to repose sank the Autumn sun;
And the crimson clouds, in the rich-hued west,
Were folding like rose-leaves round his rest.
My heart was light and I hummed a tune
As I hied me home by the harvest moon;
And I blessed her soft and gentle ray
That rose to lighten my lone pathway.

Then I thought of my Kathleen's winning smile,
(And I felt my heart grow sad the while)
Of her cheek like the fading rose-clouds glowing,
Of her hair like the dying sunlight flowing;
And her words, like the song of a summer's bird
And her air and her step like the fawn's when stirred
By the hunter's horn, all booming o'er
The woody glens of steep Slievemore.

The broad Lough Mask beneath me lay,
Like a sheet of foam in the silver ray,
And its yellow shores were round it rolled
As a gem enclosed by its fretted gold;
And there, where the old oaks mark the spot,
Arose my Kathleen's sheltered cot
And I bounded on, for my hopes were high,
Though still at heart rose the unbidden sigh.

The silver moon was veiled by a cloud,
And the darkness fell on my soul like a shroud;
And a figure in white was seen from afar,
To flit on my path like a twinkling star.
I rushed, I ran, 'twas my Kathleen dear
By why does she fly, has she aught to fear?
I called, but in vain — like the flitting beam,
She seemed to melt with the flowing stream.

I came to her father's cottage door
But the sounds of wailing were on the floor;
And the keener's voice rose loud and wild
And a mother bewailed her darling child.
My heart grew chill — I could not draw
The latch, I knew 'twas her *fetch* I saw!
Yes, Kathleen, fair Kathleen, that sad night died
The fond pulse of my soul, its hope, its pride.

64. GOOD SHOOTING

. . . He was the greatest shot that was ever in Kilmeen or
that'll ever be in it agin. One night he was sittin' be his fire
with some of the boys around him, an' a big pot of boilin'
water on the fire. All of a sudden there was a cry of wild
duck passin' overhead an' your great-grandfather — God
be good to him, he's hardly in Purgatory all these years, if
he wasn't a saint itself — an' your grandfather, as I was
sayin', jumped up an' whipped down the loaded gun that
was always hung over the chimney. He hadn't time to run
out, so he just put his head up the chimney, an' let fly, an'
be the time he had stepped out from the chimney, down
thunders as purty a goolden-winged mallard as ever bate a
wing, shot through the breast, and plunged straight into the
pot of boilin' water. So your great-grandfather put the lid
on the pot, hung up the gun, an' turnin' around to open-
mouthed neighbours about him, says, 'Boys,' he says,
'from the width yer gobs are open it must be a great hunger
that's upon ye, so we'll make a male of this little duck in the
pot before ye go — feathers an' all?' He did so, bedad. . .

65. WHO WERE THE BUILDERS

Who were the builders? Question not the silence
That settles on the lake for evermore,
Save when the sea-bird screams and to the islands
The echo answers from the steep-cliffed shore.

O half-remaining ruin, in the lore
Of human life a gap shall all deplore
Beholding thee; since thou art like the dead
Found slain, no token to reveal the why,
The name, the story. Some one murdered
We know, we guess; and gazing upon thee,
And, filled by thy long silence of reply,
We guess some garnered sheaf of tragedy; —
Or tribe or nation slain so utterly
That even their ghosts are dead, and on their grave
Springeth no bloom of legend in its wildness;
And age by age weak washing round the islands
No faintest sigh of story lisps the wave.

66. GUNRUNNING

Kilkee is seething with excitement yesterday and today, about a reported successful gunrunning coup, which, it is said, was carried out successfully in the early hours of yesterday morning between twelve and two o'clock, but it is impossible to find out details about the matter. Everyone in town is staring out to sea, looking for cruisers, and every sail seen is a ship carrying 'contraband of war'. About twelve o'clock on Tuesday the cruiser *Diamond* came close in to the entrance to the bay, and signalled to the Coastguards, also making inquiries about the Volunteer camp which is situated in the Sports field near the Coastguard Station. Last evening two warships were also seen in the offing signalling, and sudden orders were received by the Coastguards regarding the mobilisation. The Coastguards sent for cars and loaded up their effects and rifles to go to the signal station at Loop Head, where they are always stationed during the manoeuvres, and of which they have charge. They went on about five o'clock this morning. The report here is that there were twelve hundred rifles landed, but I give this for what it is worth.

67. ATHLONE

Does any man dream that a Gael can fear? —
   Of a thousand deeds let him learn but one!
The Shannon swept onward broad and clear,
   Between the leaguers and broad Athlone.

'Break down the bridge!' — Six warriors rushed
   Through the storm of shot and the storm of shell:
With late but certain victory flushed
   The grim Dutch gunners eyed them well.

They wrench'd at the planks 'mid a hail of fire:
   They fell in death, their work half done:
The bridge stood fast; and nigh and nigher
   The foe swarmed darkly, densely on.

'O, who for Erin will strike a stroke?
   Who hurl yon planks where the waters roar?'
Six warriors forth from their comrades broke,
   And flung them upon that bridge once more.

Again at the rocking planks they dashed;
   And four dropped dead; and two remained:
The huge beams groaned, and the arch down-
                      crashed;
   Two stalwart swimmers the margin gained.

St Ruth in his stirrups stood up, and cried,
   'I have seen no deed like that in France!'
With a toss of his head, Sarsfield replied,
   'They had luck, the dogs! 'Twas a merry chance!'

O many a year upon Shannon's side
   They sang upon moor and they sang upon heath
Of the twain that breasted that raging tide,
   And the ten that shook bloody hands with Death!

68. DANNY

One night a score of Erris men,
A score I'm told and nine,
Said, 'We'll get shut of Danny's noise
Of girls and widows dyin'.

'There's not his like from Binghamstown
To Boyle and Ballycroy,
At playing hell on decent girls,
At beating man and boy.

'He's left two pairs of female twins
Beyond in Killacreest,
And twice in Crossmolina fair
He's struck the parish priest.

'But we'll come round him in the night
A mile beyond the Mullet;
Ten will quench his bloody eyes,
And ten will choke his gullet.'

It wasn't long till Danny came,
From Bangor making way,
And he was damning moon and stars
And whistling grand and gay.

Till in a gap of hazel glen —
And not a hare in sight —
Out lepped the nine and twenty lads
Along his left and right.

Then Danny smashed the nose on Byrne,
He split the lips on three,
And bit across the right-hand thumb
On one Red Shawn Magee.

But seven tripped him up behind,
And seven kicked before,

And seven squeezed around his throat
Till Danny kicked no more.

Then some destroyed him with their heels,
Some tramped him in the mud,
Some stole his purse and timber pipe,
And some washed off his blood.

And when you're walking out the way
From Bangor to Belmullet,
You'll see a flat cross on a stone,
Where men choked Danny's gullet.

69. LIKENESS

The Oxford dictionary describes a *fetch* as a 'person's wraith or double'. The term had a different interpretation in old Irish lore. It was a kind of *banshee*. Like the dictionary meaning, it was similar in appearance to some person but it was a type of ghost which appeared if some disaster was about to happen. It 'had the exact form and resemblance as to air, stature, features and dress' and it appeared to a friend of the unfortunate about to die or meet with some other catastrophe.

Near the foot of Croagh Patrick lived Menee O'Malley, a charming and beautiful girl. She had the neatest cabin in the district for she had a 'great pair of hands'. She could knit, sew, tend to fowl so her mother and a host of young men loved her.

Her heart, however, belonged to a childhood sweetheart, Ulick Joyce who, while a decent, respectable lad himself, had a cousin a smuggler.

One winter's night the smuggler captured a great quantity of liquor from a ship. He called together all his neighbours and there was a great night of revelry. He watched Menee with lustful eyes as she cavorted with her loved one and when he became very drunk he made a pass at the handsome girl.

Thereafter he became obsessed with but one desire — to have Menee for his wife. But though he pestered her and gave her valuable presents she refused his offers of marriage vowing eternal love to her sweetheart.

Now the smuggler had another great haul from a ship bound for the firm of Burke, Blake, Brown, Kirwan and Company in Galway. There was brandy, gin and spice on board and as the smuggler enjoyed another evening of wine and song his thoughts turned to women and, of course, to Menee. He decided to call upon her.

Meanwhile Ulick and Manus an Omedhaun, a simple fellow, were catching trout in a mountain stream when Manus screamed and pointed to a form sitting on the river bank. It was Menee's *fetch*. They both rushed to the girl's house and found the smuggler molesting her. Ulick rushed at the smuggler and received a cut scalp from the sabre he had drawn to defend himself. The sight of his blood made Manus wild. He became a raving lunatic and rushed at the errant smuggler, grabbing him by the throat. They rolled out the door locked in combat. On they rolled and over a cliff near Murrisk. When the sea was dragged they found Manus still clinging to the smuggler's throat. Even in death he didn't let go, such was his fury.

70. AN COMHRAC

Bhí mo bhád beag iomartha ag dul le sruth na habhann, agus mé féin i mo luí ina dheireadh gan mórán aird agam ar aon rud. Níor facthas lá chomh ciúin leis go minic: gan smeámh as aer, néalta móra ómracha samhraidh sna spéartha uachtaracha agus iad go codlatach; beacha go saothrach agus go dordánach i mbéal gach bláth dá raibh ar an mbruach, plab-plab an bháid tríd an uisce ciúin ina shuantraí i mo chluais — sin a raibh le feiceáil nó le cloisteáil agam an lá buí samhraidh sin.

Leisce? Leisce agus codladh, codladh agus leisce — bhí an dá rud orm ionas go mba chuma liom cá seolfaí mo bhád nó cá bhfanfadh sí, ach mé i mo luí ansin ina tóin ar sheanchótaí agus ar shúsaí, gan aird agam ar aon rud beo nó marbh ach mé ag ligean do na smaointe fánacha teacht agus imeacht de réir a dtola.

Agus bhí cosúlacht ar mo ghadhar seilge a bhí ar an mbruach go raibh sé chomh codlatach lena mháistir: uaireanta, agus é tamall roimh an mbád, luíodh sé síos ar a shuaimhneas go mbínn féin agus an bád i dtosach air, agus ansin nuair a bhíodh sé scaitheamh romham arís d'fhanadh sé ar a shó liom dreas eile. Sócúlacht agus síocháin — ná bí ag caint ar an tsócúlacht ná ar an tsíocháin ná ar an gciúnas a bhí ann an lá fada samhraidh sin. . .

Ba dhóigh le duine, a leithéid sin de lá, nár doirteadh fuil, nár tarraingíodh claíomh, nár caitheadh gunna, nár cuireadh ionga i bhfeoil ná fiacail i gcraiceann riamh ar an saol suairc síochánta seo. . .

B'aoibhinn bheith beo a leithéid de lá, cinnte. Bhí sé de leithscéal agam go rabhas ag iascaireacht breac; ach má bhí, ní raibh ann ach leithscéal. Bhí an tsalt i mo ghlac agam, cinnte; ach má bhí, sin a raibh d'aird agam ar an iascaireacht, ach mé ag breathnú uaim go leisciúil ar bheanna Mhaigh Eo agus Dhúiche Sheoigheach a bhí ag sá na spéire ó thuaidh uaim. Scáth scamaill ag imeacht tharstu ó am go ham ar nós scamaill na feirge ar éadan duine.

Bhíos ar tí mo dhorú a ghlinneáil suas, ligean don bhád imeacht le sruth agus mo shuaimhneas a ghlacadh nuair a thugas faoi deara a chorraithe a bhí mo ghadhar seilge. Shás amach na maidí rámha, leis an mbád a choinneáil gan a dhul le sruth, ionas go bhfeichfinn céard a bhí ag cur as don mhada.

Bhí sé ina sheasamh ansin i bhfoisceacht deich slat don bhád agus cúig slat don bhruach ar ghob gainmheach giolcach báite, a bhí ag dul amach sa sruth, gan aird aige ormsa ná ar mo chuid feadaíola. Srón air, cluas air, súil air; an uile bhall dá bhaill, an uile chéadfa dá chéadfaí ar bís, é scartha leis an leisce, é chomh beo bíogach le haon ainmhí dá bhfaca duine riamh.

Saighead i mbogha, saighead a bhí ar tí a scaoilte a bhí sa ghadhar seilge sin. Scaoileadh an tsaighead go tobann. D'imigh an tsaighead sin as an mbogha le luas na gaoithe.

Corraíodh an t-uisce thart ar an ngob gainmheach giolcach báite, agus nuair d'fhéad mo shúilese a dhéanamh amach céard a bhí ar siúl bhí an gadhar mór rua i bhfostú i rud éigin san uisce tanaí i measc na ngiolcach. . .

Ann a bhí an choimhlint ansin. Ann a bhí an choraíocht. D'eirigh puiteach agus gaineamh in airde ón ngob, ionas nach bhféadfá an gadhar ná an rud a bhí ag troid leis a fheiceáil. Bhí na giolcaigh tiubh go leor thart ar an áit a raibh an troid ar siúl, agus nuair a bhaineadh ceachtar den dá ainmhí a bhí i ngreim báis ina chéile casadh as an gceann eile, chroithfí na giolcaigh seo, agus bhainfí ceol astu díreach mar chroithfí barra na gcrann i gcoill aimsir stoirme móire.

D'éirigh leis an ngadhar rua ainmhí maith mór a thabhairt i dtír tar éis tamaill fhada, ach ní rua a bhí sé an uair sin ach dath na láibe air féin agus ar an gcreach a bhí i ngreim aige.

Dobharchú a bhí aige, agus is dócha gur shíl an gadhar go raibh an beithíoch beag fíochmhar sin marbh, mar scaoil sé uaidh é ar an talamh tirim. Bhain an dobharchú casadh as féin. Shíl sé éalú leis isteac sa sruth arís. Ach níor bhronn Dia coisíocht an-mhaith air. I gceann nóiméid bhí an gadhar i bhfostú ann arís, ach má bhí d'éirigh leis an mbeithíoch beag fíochmhar a bhí i sáinn a cheann leathan íseal a chasadh thart agus na fiacla géara gearra a shá isteach i sróin dhubh an ghadhair. Scaoil an dobharchú a ghreim féin freisin agus shíl imeacht agus an t-uisce a thabhairt air féin. Ach bhí sé fánach aige. Greim scornaigh a fuair an gadhar air den chéad uair eile. Chraith sé go nimhneach é, agus fuil an dá bheithíoch measctha ar a chéile. Chroith sé in aer é. Rug arís air sular shroich sé talamh. Chroith sé agus chroith sé agus chroith sé é, go raibh an dá ainmhí chomh tugtha lena chéile, shílfeá . .

Ach ba threise an gadhar ná an dobharchú. Is mó an teacht aniar a bhí ann. Scaoil sé a ghreim go tobann ar an dobharchú, ach má scaoil rug sé arís air; greim os cionn an chroí a fuair sé air an uair seo. Cúr le béal an dá ainmhí agus iad spíonta; chloisfeá a n-anáil i gciúnas an lae — sea, chloisfeá, agus dá mbeadh cluas ghéar ort chloisfeá gíóg lag-ghlórach truamhéileach ón dobharchú freisin.

Bhí an marú déanta. . .

Sháigh an gadhar seilge a shrón in aer go mórálach. Scaoil sé aon ghlam mór fada bua uaidh go raibh an chreach marbh ag a chosa, gur chomhlíon sé a dhúchas.

71. THE WEST'S ASLEEP

When all beside a vigil keep,
The West's asleep, the West's asleep,
Alas! and well may Erin weep,
When Connacht lies in slumber deep.
There lake and plain smile fair and free,
'Mid rocks their guardian chivalry.
Sing, Oh! let man learn liberty
From crashing wind and lashing sea.

That chainless wave and lovely land
Freedom and Nationhood demand;
Be sure, the great God never planned,
For slumb'ring slaves a home so grand.
And long, a brave and haughty race
Honoured and sentinelled the place.
Sing, Oh! not even their son's disgrace
Can quite destroy their glory's trace.

For often, in O'Connor's van,
To triumph dashed each Connacht clan,
And fleet as deer the Normans ran
Thro' Corrsliabh Pass and Ardrahan;
And later times saw deeds as brave,
And glory guards Clanricarde's grave
Sing, Oh! they died their land to save
At Aughrim's slopes and Shannon's wave.

And if, when all a vigil keep,
The West's asleep; the West's asleep!
Alas! and well may Erin weep,
That Connacht lies in slumber deep,
But hark! a voice like thunder spake
'The West's awake! the West's awake!'
Sing, Oh! hurrah! let England quake,
We'll watch till death for Erin's sake!

* * * * *

Sources

1. *The Men of the West* by William Rooney.
2. From *The West and Connamara* by Mr & Mrs S. C. Hall.
3. *Lament of Mac Liag for Kincora* transl. by James Clarence Mangan.
4. From *A Queen of Men* by William O'Brien.
5. *The Boys from the County Mayo* — Anonymous. *(By permission of Walton's Limited, Dublin.)*
6. Election Address of Thomas Burke (the bonesetter), Independent candidate in the 1948 General Election.
7. *Clonmacnoise* transl. by T. W. Rolleston from the Irish of Angus O'Gillan.
8. From *The West and Connamara* by Mr & Mrs S. C. Hall.
9. *The Grave of Rury* by T. W. Rolleston.
10. From *The West and Connamara* by Mr & Mrs S. C. Hall.
11. An anonymous poem concerning a legend of the 1691 war.
12. From the paperback *The Magic of the Shannon* by John M. Feehan.
13. From *The Adventures of Donnchadh Ruadh Mac Con-Mara* transl. by Standish Hayes O'Grady under the name S. Hayes.
14. Author's condensed version of a story from Paddy Sherlock, Chimney Sweep (*Bealoideas*, Vol. V, Umh 1, *Meitheamh* 1935).
15. By Thomas D'Arcy McGee. Carolan was a renowned harpist.
16. Part of a will made by Humphrey Reynolds, Loughscur, Co. Leitrim around 1660.
17. From a manuscript in the Department of Folklore.
18. From *The Literary Writings of Patrick Pearse* by Séamas Ó Buachalla.
19. By William Rooney. Gráinne Mhaol was a flamboyant sea-pirate (Grace O'Malley) '. . . the nurse of all rebellions in Connaught'.
20. Condensed from an account contained in the *Recollections of Cormac Cahir O'Connor Faly* edited by Patrick Fahy.
21. *The County of Mayo* by George Fox.
22. A translation from *The Book of Ballymote* contained in *The Dublin Penny Journal* (1832).
23 *The Famine Year* by Lady Wilde.
24. Local history.
25. From *Ireland* by H. D. Inglis.
26. From a report by a survivor of the Spanish Armada, Francisco de Cuellar.
27. By Henry Grattan Curran Esq. from *Irish Minstrelsy or Bardic Remains of Ireland* by James Hardiman, Vol. 1.
28. From Hardiman's *History of Galway*.

29. From Hardiman's *History of Galway*.

30. *After Aughrim* by Emily Lawless.

31. *A Lamentation on Edward Walsh for the Murder of Mary Walsh Wife, of Castlebar*. From the paperback *The Mercier Book of Old Irish Street Ballads* Vol. 1, by James N. Healy.

32. Historical documentation and oral tradition.

33. *The Curse of Cromwell* or *The Desolation of the West* by Aubrey de Vere.

34. A translation from *The Book of Ballymote* contained in *The Dublin Penny Journal* (1832).

35. *The Knight of the Carpet Bag*. Anonymous ballad sometimes called *The Man from Galway*. From the paperback *The Mercier Book of Old Irish Street Ballads*, Vol. 2, by James N. Healy.

36. From *The West and Connamara* by Mr and Mrs S. C. Hall.

37. From *Lyrics of Ireland* collected by Samuel Lover and composed by a friar of the monastery in Ballyhaunis. Translation by Edward Walshe.

38. Historical documentation.

39. From *The Mercier Book of Old Irish Street Ballads*, Vol. 4, by James N. Healy.

40. From the paperback *The Short Stories of Padraic Pearse* by Desmond Maguire.

41. From the paperback *The Mercier Book of Old Irish Street Ballads*, Vol. 1, by James N. Healy.

42. From *Irish Freedom* September 1911.

43. By William Rooney from the paperback *The Third Book of Irish Ballads* by Maureen Jolliffe.

44. From *A Little Tour of Ireland* by S. Reynolds Hole.

45. *A Lament Written On the Dreadful Massacre of Six-Mile-Bridge, in the County Clare*. From *The Mercier Book of Old Irish Street Ballads*, Vol. 2, by James N. Healy.

46. From Hardiman's *History of Galway*.

47. From the paperback *First Book of Irish Ballads*, by Daniel D. O'Keeffe, with notes and music by James N. Healy.

48. From *Roscommon Herald* 11 November 1893.

49. Historical Documentation.

50. From *The Playboy of the Western World* by J. M. Synge.

51. *The Song of O'Ruark, Prince of Breffni* by Thomas Moore.

52. From the paperback *Rambles in the West of Ireland* by William Bulfin.

53. From *The Mercier Book of Old Irish Street Ballads*, Vol. 1, by James N. Healy.

54. Verse used for Gaelic League advertising in 1918.

55. Condensed from a folk tale in the manuscript collection of the Department of Folklore at University College, Dublin.

56. From *The Mercier Book of Old Irish Street Ballads*, Vol. 3, by James N. Healy.

57. From *Ireland* by H. D. Inglis.

58. From *Prose, Poems and Parodies* by Percy French.

59. Condensed from a folktale in *Duffy's Fireside Magazine*, Vol. 1.

60. From the paperback *Percy French and his Songs* by James N. Healy.

61. Oral tradition.

62. From the paperback *Percy French and his Songs* by James N. Healy.

63. From *Dublin Penny Journal* 26 April 1834.

64. From *The Leprechaun of Killmeen* by Seamus O'Kelly.

65. *The Nameless Doon* by William Larminie.

66. From the *Clare Journal* 30 July 1914.

67. *A Ballad of Athlone (Second Siege)*, or *How They Broke Down the Bridge* by Aubrey de Vere.

68. From *Plays, Poems and Prose* by John Millington Synge.

69. From *Duffy's Fireside Magazine*, April 1834.

70. From *Beagnac Fíor* by Padraic Ó Conaire.

71. By Thomas Davis.